OLD-EARTH
CREATIONISM
ON TRIAL

THE VERDICT IS IN

TIM CHAFFEY & JASON LISLE

Master
Books

TIM CHAFFEY & JASON LISLE

OLD-EARTH
CREATIONISM
ON TRIAL

THE VERDICT IS IN

First printing: June 2008
Third printing: August 2010

ISBN-13: 978-0-89051-544-0
ISBN-10: 0-89051-544-1
Library of Congress Number: 2008928493

Unless otherwise noted, all Scripture is from the New King James
Version of the Bible.

Please consider requesting that a copy of this volume be purchased by
your local library system.

Printed in the United States of America

Please visit our website for other great titles:
www.masterbooks.net

For information regarding author interviews,
please contact the publicity department at (870) 438-5288.

Master
Books®
A Division of New Leaf Publishing Group
www.masterbooks.net

Acknowledgments

We would like to thank the many people who have helped make this book a reality.

Pastor and English teacher Glenn Andes, for taking time out of his busy schedule to proofread the manuscript and for his encouragement.

Our colleagues at Answers in Genesis and the Institute for Creation Research for their tireless efforts to glorify God by standing up for the truth of His Word (especially in Genesis).

Bodie Hodge and Terry Mortenson for reviewing various sections of the book.

Our families, for their support and encouragement.

Finally, and most importantly, we want to thank the Lord Jesus Christ for saving us from our sins and giving us a strong desire to uphold the authority, authenticity, and accuracy of His Word. We pray that He will be glorified through this book.

Table of Contents

Preface

Young-earth creationists and old-earth creationists have been debating their respective positions for two centuries. The controversy has become one of the major battles in the modern church. In this book, *young-earth creationists* are defined as Christians who believe God created everything during a six-day period of time about six thousand years ago.[1] These days are to be understood as approximately 24 hours in length. *Old-earth creationists* are defined as Christians who believe God created everything during the course of the past several billion years. It is important to understand that young-earth creationists do not necessarily agree with each other on every point and old-earth creationists do not agree with each other on every point.

Both sides appeal to the Scriptures for support. However, as will be demonstrated, many of the arguments used by the old-earth creationists do not stand up to scrutiny. Young-earth creationists have often supplied responses to these arguments, but it seems these responses are often ignored and the poor arguments persist. One of the goals of this book is to call attention to the faulty and sometimes misleading argumentation that exists in this debate.

The young-earth creationists' responses typically take one of two forms. First, brief articles designed to refute a particular claim are published in magazines or on websites. Second, a book is written to respond to the views of a particular old-earth creationist or to seriously critique certain arguments pertaining to one area of research.

---

1. Some young-earth creationists allow for the possibility of gaps in the Genesis genealogies. By doing this, they allow for an extra four thousand years or so. *See Appendix C for information on the idea of gaps in the genealogies.*

This book is unique in that it provides a thorough biblical, theological, and scientific critique of old-earth creationism while maintaining its readability. Many of the books designed to refute old-earth creationism contain a great deal of technical jargon and remain above the head of the average layperson. We have consciously endeavored to avoid this language as much as possible in this book. To help the reader when these terms do arise, such terms will be defined in text boxes on the first page in which they appear. Also, for those who are looking for more detail on a given subject, this book is documented so that readers can easily find more information. Appendix F is provided for readers looking for specific young-earth scientific arguments that are beyond the scope of this book.

Although the scientific evidence certainly bears weight in the debate between these two camps, this work focuses mainly on biblical and theological arguments. After all, from a Christian perspective, if one side cannot support its view from Scripture, then it cannot be the proper view. Nonetheless, it is important to show that good science does support the biblical time scale. For this reason, we will deal with the philosophy and application of science and how evidence is interpreted in chapters 7 and 8.

To deal with this subject, two major areas must be covered. First and foremost, the age of the earth must be examined. Does the Bible teach a young age (approximately 6,000 years) for the earth (and universe) or does it support the idea that the age of our planet is about 4.5 billion years and that of the universe about 14 billion years? Second, the flood of Noah's day must be studied in detail. If the Flood waters covered the entire earth, then a severe blow is dealt to the old-earth creationism camp. However, the converse is also true. If the Flood only covered a region of the planet, then young-earth creationism has no mechanism to explain the geologic features of the world. Furthermore, if the Flood was a global event, then the young-earth creationists' claim that Genesis 1–11 should be interpreted as straightforward, literal history is strongly supported.

Since this is such an important debate, suggestions for improving the debate are provided for both sides. God will be honored when both "old-earthers" and "young-earthers" engage in honest debate rather than resorting to misrepresentation, ambiguity, straw-man arguments, and caustic language. It is our hope that this book will serve to clarify the debate by giving an up-to-date defense of the young-earth view and by exposing the many fallacious arguments used in defense of the old-earth views.

Above all, both sides must remember that God's Word is inspired, inerrant, and authoritative. It is our responsibility to faithfully proclaim His Word to an unbelieving world. God stated in Isaiah 55:11:

> So shall My word be that goes forth from My mouth; it shall not return to Me void, but it shall accomplish what I please, and it shall prosper in the thing for which I sent it.

The primary goal of this work is to call the Church back to the authority of Scripture rather than trusting our own methods and ideas (Ps. 118:8). May God stir you to develop a deeper love and trust for His Word and His Son.

Chapter 1

An Introduction

The early 19th century witnessed a dramatic shift in the Church's hermeneutical approach with respect to the early chapters of Genesis.[1] Prior to this time, the majority of Christians believed the Bible taught that God created the world around six thousand years ago. As the scientific community began promulgating the view of a much older earth, Christians began searching the Bible to see if it permitted one to accept these new dates for the age of the earth. Various theories were proposed, such as the *gap theory* and the *day-age theory.*

> *Hermeneutics —*
> *the study of the*
> *methodological*
> *principles of*
> *interpretation (as of*
> *the Bible).*

Throughout the past two centuries, these theories have been tweaked, while others have been created. Some Christians have gone so far as to promote *theistic evolution,* a view that teaches that God used evolution as His means of creation. However, among conservative scholarship, biological evolution is generally denied in favor of views that promote the special creation of man and woman. Today, the

---

1. See Dr. Terry Mortenson's *The Great Turning Point* (Green Forest, AR: Master Books, 2004) for a history of the geological and biblical battles of the early 19th century.

framework hypothesis and *progressive creation* are popular among theologians and Christian scientists. (See Appendix A for a description of these and other views.)

With the resurgence of young-earth creationism in recent decades, the debate over the age of the earth and the proper hermeneutical approach to Genesis has intensified within evangelical circles. Scholars on both sides of the dispute have written at length in an effort to convince the Church, which is largely uninformed on the issue. In their zeal to convince others, many of these scholars have resorted to weak and oftentimes fallacious arguments and reasoning.

For years, Answers in Genesis has been cautioning young-earth creationists to utilize more discretion when promoting arguments that seemingly advance their view. An article on their website lists numerous popular arguments that they suggest should not be used.[2] This opened the door for criticism from fellow young-earthers who had used these arguments or supported ministries that did. Nevertheless, this article was sorely needed and demonstrated how important it is for believers to be more interested in truth than winning the public's approval.

All ideas and theories should be subjected to rigorous self-examination, yet a similar self-critique is long overdue from the old-earth creationists. Since such a critique is not forthcoming from the old-earthers, one will be offered here.

The following chapters will loosely follow the procedures of a court case. First, the prosecution (young-earthers) will make its case regarding the age of the earth from a biblical perspective. Here, a summary of young-earth creationists' biblical and theological arguments will be listed to illustrate what the old-earth creationists are responding to. Second, the defense will have their say. In this section, the old-earthers' responses to these arguments will be categorized and summarized. Each of these responses will be treated like a witness in court in that they will be immediately cross-examined in light of Scripture. This will serve to illustrate the extremely shaky theological ground occupied by the old-earth position.

---

2. Available at www.answersingenesis.org/home/area/faq/dont_use.asp; accessed May 27, 2008.

Following the first round of proceedings, the debate over the extent of the flood in Noah's day will be examined in the same manner. The young-earthers' arguments for a worldwide flood will be given followed by the old-earthers' responses and a biblical cross-examination.

Finally, the scientific evidence will be evaluated. This too will be examined in light of the teachings of Scripture. The Bible alone provides the philosophical foundation for logical thought and scientific inquiry. The Bible also provides a strategy for the logical refutation of false claims. Using the biblical strategy, we will explore scientific arguments for a young earth. In the following chapter, scientific arguments used to support an old earth will be examined.

Why Do Christians Keep Fighting about This Issue When They Should Be Focused on the Gospel?

As young-earth creationists, we hear this question often. There are undoubtedly several reasons why this question is being asked. Numerous believers do not understand the importance of this battle and as a result, are turned off by the ongoing debate over the correct interpretation of Genesis 1–11. They see it as a distraction to a church that needs to be focused on leading the lost to Christ. While these believers have good intentions, we believe they have not thought enough about the importance of the debate.

First and foremost, God included these 11 chapters in His Word, so He expects us to know and understand them. Christians do not have the freedom to pick and choose which parts of the Bible are important to know and which are not. It is certainly true that some portions of Scripture have more application to the Christian than other portions, but all Scripture is important.

Second, many people do not understand the foundational nature of this debate. If the young-earth interpretation is the correct one (and this will be demonstrated throughout the remainder of the book), then Christians dare not abandon the proper interpretation. This is especially true when it comes to the study of origins. After all, what a person believes about his or her origins has a drastic impact on the way he or she lives. Moreover, if Genesis 1–11 can be reinterpreted, then all biblical interpretation is suspect since the Bible writers repeatedly

> *Exegesis — an accurate and critical interpretation of a text. This is contrary to eisegesis, which occurs when a person attempts to fit their thoughts into the text.*

treated Genesis 1–11 as real history, as will be shown later.

Third, many Christians (unfortunately) see logical reasoning and careful exegesis as antithetical to faith. To them, it is not important to have answers on these kinds of issues; they seem to prefer having a "blind faith." We often hear statements like, "Don't worry about these issues, just trust in Jesus." Now, don't misunderstand; of course we should trust in Jesus. But our trust should not be a "blind faith." In other words, we should not simply trust for the sake of trusting or because of some emotional experience (otherwise our faith will be no different than any other religion). Rather, we trust in Christ because He proved He is God by rising from the dead. We trust in the Bible because it has demonstrated itself to be reliable time and again.

Our faith is not "blind." Our trust in God's Word is not *despite* careful analysis, but rather *because* of it! Scripture is clear that God expects His people to study and think. Paul set the example for us as he went to synagogue after synagogue and reasoned with the Jews from the Scriptures that Jesus is the Messiah (Acts 17:2–3, 18:4). God challenged His rebellious people to "Come now, and let us reason together" (Isa. 1:18). It is not sinful for Christians to have sincere questions about their faith. God is up to the challenge, and His Word will provide the answers. We should be like the Bereans, who were commended by Luke because they "searched the Scriptures daily" (Acts 17:11).

Young-earth creationists are often asked why they feel it is necessary to correct fellow believers and refute their ideas about an old earth. First, we care about the old-earth creationists. It would be irresponsible and unloving to ignore serious errors promoted by our brothers and sisters in Christ and allow them to go down a path that is ultimately unbiblical. We Christians must always challenge each other to be faithful to the text of Scripture. We should welcome constructive criticism.

Second, why is this question seldom asked of the old-earther who does the same to the young-earther? We are often labeled as divisive when we talk about the importance of believing in a young earth.

However, it should be remembered that it was the old-earth creationists who divided the Church in the early 19th century by bringing in a concept foreign to the Scriptures and contrary to 18 centuries of orthodox belief. We are simply trying to call the Church back to the authority of God's Word. If this is divisive, then it certainly illustrates how far the Church has come from biblical truth. Our goal is to unite around sound doctrine, not to haggle over minor issues. Jude instructed believers to "contend earnestly for the faith" (Jude 3) and this is what we believe young-earthers are attempting to do.

> *Orthodox* — *teachings historically accepted as authentic by the Church.*
>
> *Heterodox* — *teachings contrary to orthodoxy.*

How Should Both Sides Treat Each Other?

This issue, like many in the Church, is emotionally charged. As such, it is very easy for people to have their feelings hurt when someone disagrees with their position. It is a very natural tendency to be defensive when our deeply held views are challenged. But we must all resist this temptation and pursue the truth, and be willing to change our thinking when and where we are shown to be in error.

Christians need to keep in mind that debate, even on emotional and controversial issues, can lead to tremendous spiritual growth for the Church. This concept is hard for many Christians to grasp because they have been raised in a "Can't we all just get along?" atmosphere in the Church. The answer to that question is an emphatic *yes!* We can get along but we do not always agree on everything. When disagreements do arise, we need to handle them with a spirit of gentleness and respect.

Church history is filled with controversial debates, and for that we should be grateful. Many of the heterodox issues that come up from time to time have already been argued and debated. For example, some early Christians were not sure how to handle the person of Jesus Christ. Was He fully God? Was He fully man? If He was God, could He really have been tempted to sin (Matt. 4:1–11)? Why did He not know the timing of His coming (Matt. 24:36)? If He was just a man, then how could He claim to be one with God (John 10:30)? The early Church debated this issue at the Council of Nicaea in A.D. 325. A popular teacher named Arius had begun teaching that Jesus was a created being rather than the eternal, omnipotent God that orthodox Christianity had always affirmed. He made some very persuasive arguments to support his case. Thankfully, Athanasius, who defended the deity of Christ, was able to point out the errors in Arius' teachings and the Council overwhelmingly sided with Athanasius. They affirmed the fact that Jesus Christ was fully God and fully man, just as the Bible teaches. Nowadays, when teachings similar to Arius' are circulated, such as the doctrine of the Jehovah's Witnesses, Christians have confidence that they have the correct view because that battle was already fought and won so many years ago.

Several other examples could be cited. The battles are still going on in various areas, and the old earth versus young earth debate is certainly one of the hottest and most important battles today. Readers must keep in mind two crucial points. First, the doctrine of Arius was extremely dangerous. After all, if Jesus Christ was not really God, then He could not have been the Savior. Arius' views must be considered heretical since they strike at the heart of the person and work of Christ. Second, the old earth versus young earth debate, as portrayed in this book, is a family matter. This is a battle between fellow believers and it bears repeating that both sides need to treat each other with respect.

Christians need to understand that disagreements happen. Sometimes these are private and sometimes they are public. Sometimes the way to handle these differences is in print. Young-earth creationists are often asked, "Why don't you just write to Dr. So-and-so (an old-earth creationist) and work out your differences in private? In Matthew 18, doesn't Jesus tell us to handle our differences with fellow believers in that way?" Yes and no. The pattern set forth in Matthew 18 is applicable when one believer sins against another believer. This is a private matter and should be handled privately — at least the first step. However, when a believer makes public statements, whether in lectures or in print, then these statements should be handled publicly. Our Lord set the example of this type of public critique when He dealt with the teachings of the Pharisees (see Matt. 23, for example). Also, the apostle Paul publicly confronted Peter (Gal. 2) and provided the names of individuals who were guilty of teaching error (2 Tim. 2:17–18).

As you read this book, keep in mind that several old-earth creationists will be quoted. We will do our best to represent the authors' intentions (and not to pull their comments out of context) so that they are being treated fairly. Also, please understand that neither their Christian commitment nor their motives are in question here. For example, one old-earther that is frequently cited is Dr. Norman Geisler. We have great respect for this Christian scholar. His writings and lectures have been a wonderful blessing to many. In no way do we wish to demean or attack him as a person or as a Christian; however, we must take issue with some of his teachings on this topic. We plead with the readers to keep these things in mind as they read this book. Also, we truly believe that many old-earthers have a zeal for reaching the lost and that they believe that their methods are the best way to do this. We do not question the sincerity of their zeal.

It's Not about Darwin

A large percentage of Christians have been led to believe that the debate over creation vs. evolution concerns Charles Darwin and natural selection. While it is true that much of the focus has been on whether biological evolution is possible, the real debate for the Church has very little to do with Darwin at all. In fact, the problem for the Church began about half a century before Darwin wrote *Origin of Species*. And today, most evangelical Christians reject Neo-Darwinian evolution.

In the late 18th century and early 19th century, the discipline of geology was in its infancy. During this time, several early geologists began to propose an age of the earth that vastly exceeded the biblical time frame accepted by nearly every Christian and Jew up until that time. One of the key figures in this development was Charles Lyell, whose *Principles of Geology* (1830–33) would have a profound effect on Darwin during his famous five-year voyage on the *H.M.S. Beagle*. As these old-earth ideas gained popularity, certain Christian leaders began to devise theories that they believed would allow them to blend the Bible with the growing opinion of geologists. As a result, the gap theory, day-age theory, and local flood theory were promoted long before Darwin's book, *Origin of Species* (1859), was ever written.

The importance of these facts cannot be overlooked because it is not Darwin's theorizing that has done the most damage to the Church. The Church has inflicted the most damage on itself by compromising with unbiblical ideas. Because Genesis began to be reinterpreted, more people started to doubt the validity of the rest of God's Word.

Jesus told Nicodemus that if He could not be trusted when He spoke about earthly things, then it would make little sense to trust Him when He spoke about heavenly affairs (John 3:12). The text of Genesis is God-breathed (2 Tim. 3:16). If believers cannot trust God's Word when it comes to the creation account, then they should have no reason to believe it when it speaks of Jesus being the only way to the Father (John 14:6). Millions of people have made this logical connection and sadly refuse to trust in Christ because they do not believe the Bible is true from the very beginning. Ultimately, the issue is not about creation versus evolution or even young earth versus old earth. It really comes down to whether or not a person can trust the Word of God from the very first verse to the very last verse. Old-earth creationists certainly claim that the battle is not over the trustworthiness of Scripture but the interpretation of it. However, the following chapters will show that the battle is truly over the trustworthiness of God's Word.

A Few Comments about Science

We will deal with the philosophy of science in chapters 7 and 8; however, a few preliminary comments are in order. Science is a powerful tool that the Lord has given us, and young-earth creationists love science. Indeed, modern science has confirmed many of the truths taught in Scripture. Some evolutionists have said that creationists reject science because we do not accept the notion of particles-to-people evolution. Likewise, some old-earth creationists accuse young-earthers of rejecting science because we do not accept the big-bang model and the generally accepted dates for the age of the earth and universe. (Please see Appendix E to see why Christians should not accept the big-bang model.) For example, the following argument can be found on a popular old-earth creationist website:

It could also be argued that ALL scientists accept an old earth. I use the word "all" because young earth scientists are not scientists. By definition, a scientist makes observations, then formulates theories about those observations. By contrast, a YEC [young-earth creationist] "scientist" has made the theory first (that the earth is young) and then he looks for observations to confirm it. They are performing science backwards, thus deserve the term "theorist" rather than "scientist."[3]

What the writer of this article fails to realize is that scientific evidence does not "speak for itself" — it requires interpretation. We all interpret evidence according to our worldview — we all have preconceived notions. Both young-earthers and old-earthers use their worldview to help them make sense of the data. Old-earth creationists use "old-earth" preconceptions when they interpret all evidence (even biblical) from an old-earth perspective. (We'll see how this works in detail in chapters 7 and 8.)

In the same article, the writer responded to a question about why he attacks young-earth creationism. He stated it was because "the earth is 4.5 billion years old, and the universe more than 13 billion years old." This writer has already accepted the opinion of the majority of scientists as true and interprets all data through that framework. Even Albert Einstein, one of the greatest scientific minds of the 20th century, stated:

> But on principle, it is quite wrong to try founding a theory on observable magnitudes alone. In reality the very opposite happens. It is the theory which decides what we can observe.[4]

A bias is not always a bad thing. A correct worldview (or bias) will enhance our ability to correctly interpret evidence (just as an incorrect one will hamper our ability). This is why it is so important to base our thinking on God's infallible Word. Every person has a worldview and

---

3. http://www.answersincreation.org/bookreview/compromise/refuting_compromise.htm. This comment is repeatedly made on the Answers in Creation website.
4. Quoted in Werner Heisenberg, *Physics and Beyond*, Arnold J. Pomerans, trans. (New York: Harper and Row, 1971), p. 63.

> **Cosmogony** — *a theory of the origin of the universe.*

will inevitably interpret data through that filter whether they realize it or not. Therefore, it is very important to make sure we have the *right* worldview: that we start with correct, biblical assumptions when we approach science — as we will discuss in chapter 7.

In reality, young-earth creationists take issue with the old-earthers' interpretation of the scientific evidence. Both sides study the same evidence. They have the same earth, stars, rocks, trees, fossils, etc. Young-earthers are not anti-science, as evidenced by the number of young-earthers who hold advanced degrees in science. Many of these scientists became young-earth creationists as a result of their scientific research.[5] The anti-science claim is nothing more than an attempt to shift the focus away from the real debate, which can only be resolved ultimately through a proper understanding of God's inerrant Word.

Moreover, young-earth creationists are not alone in their rejection of the popular scientific theories of the day. Many scientists do not agree with the *status quo* of the scientific community. While the majority may accept the old-earth view, they disagree over the means of how this world came about. For example, 34 secular scientists recently published an open letter calling for the need to research alternative cosmogonies because they believe the big bang is fraught with too many insurmountable scientific problems.[6] At present, five hundred scientists have signed on, affirming their agreement with the letter. This letter calls for a more balanced allocation of funding, since they believe billions of dollars are being wasted in trying to keep a dying theory alive. The fact of the matter is that the scientific evidence does not necessarily lend as much support for an old earth as old-earthers often imply.

---

5. A good overview of this topic can be found in John Ashton, *In Six Days* (Green Forest, AR: Master Books, 2003). This book is a compilation of the testimonies of 50 scientists explaining why they are young-earth creationists.
6. E.J. Lerner et al., "An Open Letter to the Scientific Community," *New Scientist* (May 22, 2004), p. 20, also at: <http://www.cosmologystatement.org>.

Chapter 2

Prosecution — Biblical Age for the Earth

Welcome to the trial of the century, or better, the trial of the last three centuries. This particular battle has been raging since the early 19th century. Arguments have been promoted in every conceivable media outlet: newspapers, books, magazines, the Internet, television, and video programs. Hopefully, after examining the arguments, the reader will see that there can only be one correct interpretation of Genesis 1–11. That interpretation is known as young-earth creationism.[1] Consider the following summary of the young-earthers' major arguments.

The Plain Teaching of Scripture

Young-earth creationists have argued that their position is the clear teaching of God's Word. The Bible teaches that God created everything in six days, and that Adam was created on the sixth day. The genealogies recorded in Scripture indicate that Abraham lived about 2,000 years after Adam was created. And since Abraham lived about 4,000 years ago, this means the earth is about 6,000 years old. The

---

1. We actually prefer the term "biblical creation," since our view of origins is determined by strict adherence to a straightforward reading of the Bible. But since we have not yet established this, we will use the term "young-earth" creation to contrast our position with those who hold to "old-earth" creation.

earth could be much older if and only if there were substantial gaps in the genealogies, or if God had taken much longer than six days to create. One young-earther put it this way:

> Taking Genesis 1 in this way, at face value, without doubt it says that God created the universe, the earth, the sun, moon and stars, plants and animals, and the first two people within six ordinary (approximately 24-hour) days. Being really honest, you would have to admit that you could never get the idea of millions of years from reading this passage.[2]

This statement offers an accurate summary of the young-earthers' claims on this point. The Bible should be allowed to speak for itself. If it states that God made everything in six literal days, then it does not matter that the majority of scientists disagree with it.

Some old-earthers admit that this is a major strength of young-earth creationism but still adhere to an old-earth interpretation because of their acceptance of modern scientific theories concerning the age of the earth. Biology Professor Pattle Pun of Wheaton College stated:

> It is apparent that the most straightforward understanding of Genesis, without regard to the hermeneutical considerations suggested by science, is that God created the heavens and the earth in six solar days, that man was created on the sixth day, and that death and chaos entered the world after the fall of Adam and Eve, and that all fossils were the result of the catastrophic deluge that spared only Noah's family and the animals therewith.[3]

Pun is not alone in making this type of claim. The late Dr. Gleason Archer, an Old Testament scholar, wrote:

> From a superficial reading, the impression received is that the entire creative process took place in six twenty-four hour days. If this was the true intent of the Hebrew author

---

2. Ken Ham, ed., *The New Answers Book* (Green Forest, AR: Master Books, 2006), p. 89.
3. P.P.T. Pun, *Journal of the American Scientific Affiliation* 39:14, 1987.

(a questionable deduction, as will be presently shown), this seems to run counter to modern scientific research, which indicates that the planet Earth was created several billion years ago.[4]

Notice that both of these men agree that the plain reading of the text is that God created everything in six ordinary days. It is only because of the "hermeneutical considerations suggested by science" that they will not accept the plain words of Scripture. This is a dangerous approach to the Bible and will be dealt with later.

In addition to this concept of the plain reading of the text, young-earth creationists point to Exodus 20:11.

> For in six days the LORD made the heavens and the earth, the sea, and all that is in them, and rested the seventh day. Therefore the LORD blessed the Sabbath day and hallowed it.

This passage is found in the midst of the Ten Commandments. God told the Israelites that the reason they were supposed to work six days and rest on the seventh is because that is precisely what He did during the creation week. Some old-earth creationists interpret each of the days of creation as long ages (many millions of years each), rather than ordinary days. But Exodus 20:11 precludes this possibility. It would be silly to think that we are supposed to work for six long ages (millions of years each) and then rest for one long age. This statement is repeated in Exodus 31:17 and in this passage we are told that God wrote the words himself. It is important to point out that the word used for "day" in these passages is the same as the word used in Genesis 1.

"Yom" in Context

This brings us to the next argument. A major point of contention centers on the definition of the word *day* in Genesis 1 and 2. Just like the English word "day," the Hebrew word *yom* (םוי) can refer to the daylight portion of a day, a 24-hour period, or an indefinite period of time. The proper interpretation is dependent upon context and is usually not too

---

4. Gleason L. Archer, *A Survey of Old Testament Introduction* (Chicago, IL: Moody, 1985), p. 187.

difficult to discern. This is true even when the same word is used multiple times in the same passage. To illustrate this point, we could make this statement, "Back in my grandfather's day, it took ten days to drive across America during the day." It is easy to understand how the word "day" is used in all three instances. Why is it that no theologian disputes whether the Israelites marched around Jericho for seven days or seven thousand years? It is because the particular context demands that *yom* in Joshua 6:14–15 is referring to a 24-hour time period.

Young-earth creationists often point out that every time *yom* is paired with the words "evening" or "morning," it refers to an ordinary day. For that matter, the phrase "evening and morning" by itself would constitute an ordinary day. When the word "night" is paired with *yom*, it also refers to an ordinary day. Whenever *yom* is used in the Old Testament with either a cardinal number or an ordinal number, it always means a literal day. In Genesis 1, *yom* appears with a cardinal number on the first day and with ordinal numbers on the second through sixth days. It also appears with the words "evening" and "morning" on all six days and the word "night" on the first day.

> **Cardinal number** — *the name given to number words (one, two, three, etc.).*
>
> **Ordinal number** — *a number designating a place in a numbered sequence (first, second, third, etc.).*

Any one of these contextual clues would be sufficient to indicate that the days of creation are ordinary days. Yet, Genesis 1 uses all of them. It seems as if God really stressed this fact to make sure we understand the days are literal, ordinary days.

Genealogical Evidence

Since Adam was created just days after the earth, the length of time between the creation of Adam and today is the approximate age of the earth. A natural reading of the biblical genealogies reveals that the earth could not be billions of years old. Genesis 5 gives a record from Adam to Noah, and Genesis 11 provides the line from Noah to Abraham. Scholars generally agree that Abraham lived around 2000 B.C. The genealogies of Genesis 5 and 11 add roughly another 2,000 years. When one adds the 2,000 years since Christ, we get an age for the earth of about 6,000 years. The old-earther is forced to try to insert numerous gaps into the text when there is strong evidence against such gaps. (For a more thorough discussion of this subject please see Appendix C.) Even if such gaps existed, they couldn't involve more than a few thousand years without making the genealogies meaningless and ludicrous. They certainly would not allow for the billions of years to be inserted. So adding gaps does not harmonize the Bible with old-earth geological and cosmological theories.

Death and Suffering before Sin

Young-earth creationists also point to several theological difficulties and contradictions created when one attempts to insert vast ages into the Genesis record. The most serious error is that this practice necessarily places death, disease, and bloodshed before sin. If there are fossils that are hundreds of millions of years old (as old-earthers believe), then those animals must have died *before* Adam sinned (since we all agree that Adam was not around millions of years ago). Some fossils have evidence of disease in them, such as cancer, arthritis, and tooth disease.

By inserting billions of years into the Bible, the old-earth view places death and suffering before sin (and therefore death and suffering could not be the result of Adam's sin). In the process, this undermines the foundation of the Gospel message itself. Old-earthers are not being accused of denying the Gospel, but their view necessarily undermines the foundation of the Gospel message. If animal death and bloodshed occurred before sin, then God pronounced these as "very good" in Genesis 1:31. If millions of years had occurred, then the curse pronounced on the animals and the ground (Gen. 3:14 and 3:17) had no effect — there was already animal death and disease and the ground was already producing thorns and thistles. Thorns and thistles are found in fossil layers that old-earth geologists say existed 300–400 million years before man came on the scene.[5] Yet, the Bible teaches that thorns and

---

5. Wilson N. Stewart and Gar W. Rothwell, *Paleobotany and the Evolution of Plants* (Cambridge, UK: Cambridge University Press, 1993), p. 172–176. It shows fossilized thorny plants (*Psilophyton crenulatum*) found in the Devonian formation, which the evolutionists date at 345–395 million years BP (before present). Also, roses are said to have evolved around 40 million years ago.

thistles are the result of sin — part of God's curse on the ground *after* Adam sinned (Gen. 3:18).

The idea that death existed prior to Adam's sin is also refuted by the original diets prescribed for both man and animals in Genesis 1:29–30.

> And God said, "See, I have given you every herb that yields seed which is on the face of all the earth, and every tree whose fruit yields seed; to you it shall be for food. Also, to every beast of the earth, to every bird of the air, and to everything that creeps on the earth, in which there is life, I have given every green herb for food"; and it was so.

Why would God command a vegetarian diet for all living creatures? The obvious answer is because death was not a part of the original creation. People were not supposed to kill animals and animals were not to kill each other. In some cases, we find fossils of animal parts *inside* other animals; the fossil record does contain abundant evidence of meat-eating animals. From the Scriptures, we know that this carnivorous behavior among some animals must have come after sin, as a result of the Curse. So, the fossils cannot be millions of years old.

What Does the New Testament Teach?

When Jesus Christ was in His earthly ministry, He confirmed that the earth is young. When questioned by the Pharisees concerning divorce, He replied, "But from the beginning of the creation, God 'made them male and female' " (Mark 10:6; Matt. 19:4). The obvious implication here is Jesus knew that Adam and Eve were created "from the beginning." If billions of years had passed prior to their creation, then Jesus' claim that Adam and Eve were from the beginning of creation would simply be wrong. The only possible way for our Lord's response to be accurate is if the days of creation were literal 24-hour days. Adam and Eve were created on the sixth day of the very first week (which would be the beginning from Jesus' vantage point 4,000 years later) — not 14 billion years after the beginning.

The New Testament contains other similar statements. For example, Romans 1:20 states:

For since the creation of the world His invisible attributes are clearly seen, being understood by the things that are made, even His eternal power and Godhead, so that they are without excuse.

While reading this verse, Christians usually focus on the concept that general revelation reveals God's attributes (or characteristics). Certainly this is taught here. But there is another interesting point about that general revelation. It states that God's attributes are clearly seen and understood "since the creation of the world." This important point cannot be emphasized enough. In order for His attributes to be "clearly seen" and "understood" since the creation of the world, someone had to be there to do the seeing and understanding. This someone does not refer to angels. The entire context of this passage deals with mankind. In other words, Paul is saying that men were around since the beginning of creation, and they were able to clearly see God's invisible attributes. This is only possible from the young-earth perspective. If billions of years had passed before man came on the scene, then Paul, inspired by the Holy Spirit, was gravely mistaken.

Restoration of Paradise

Isaiah 65:25 prophesied of a peaceful time when "the wolf and the lamb shall feed together" and "the lion shall eat straw like the ox." This restoration hearkens back to the original creation when all animals were vegetarian (Gen. 1:30). This is problematic for the old-earth creationist because he does not believe that all creatures were originally vegetarian. Recall that evidence of meat-eating creatures is found in the fossil record. Since the old-earther believes these fossils are millions of years old, he is forced to believe that carnivorous activity existed long before the time of Adam. But this runs contrary to Genesis 1:30.

In the future, God will create "a new heaven and a new earth" (Rev. 21:1). To our knowledge, no Christian believes this will take God billions of years to create. Why then insist that it took this long the first time?

Several other theological problems could be listed, as well as scores of scientific difficulties, but these will suffice to give a summary of the young-earth creationist's major biblical arguments. Also, some of the other young-earth arguments will surface during the next few chapters. It is time to examine the old-earthers' responses to these points and see if they can stand up to the scrutiny of a biblical cross-examination.

Chapter 3

Defense — "Biblical" Arguments

A s will be demonstrated, old-earth creationists have a difficult time responding to the arguments mentioned in the previous chapter. Several well-known evangelical leaders have offered arguments against young-earth creationism. It is surprising to see the very inadequate responses from otherwise brilliant men. Sadly, many old-earth creationists knowingly misrepresent young-earth creationism, while others resort to *ad hominem* arguments, straw-man attacks, and other fallacious debate tactics. This chapter will focus specifically on their attempts to respond from Scripture. The following chapter will highlight their faulty argumentation and poor theological reasoning.

Rewriting the Rules of Interpretation

To open their defense, the old-earth creationists have used an approach that has gained some acceptance over the past century. Simply stated, some old-earth creationists have sought to reconcile the apparent conflict between science and Scripture by changing hermeneutical guidelines. In other words, according to old-earthers, it seems that the general rules of interpretation just do not apply to Genesis. Instead, it should be treated differently than any other book.

> **Historical-Grammatical**
> — *The standard conservative method of interpretation that seeks to find the author's intended meaning.*

A. Berkeley Mickelsen authored a comprehensive textbook on hermeneutics. In an otherwise outstanding work, Mickelsen advocated that a unique approach be applied to the Genesis text. He also includes the Book of Revelation in this interpretive scheme and says these two books use "the language of creation and climax."[1] He writes, "the age of the universe, the nature of light, [and] the time and procedures by which God prepared the earth for habitation of man are not touched upon at all [in the Bible]."[2] By applying the standard historical-grammatical hermeneutic to Genesis, it is easy to see that Mickelsen is simply wrong. First, the age of the universe can be calculated to within a few generations by adding up the ages given in the genealogies. Even if we allow for gaps in the genealogies, it is most unreasonable to try to fit tens of thousands of years or more into the record.[3] Second, it has already been shown that it took God five ordinary days plus a part of the sixth day to prepare the earth for the "habitation of man." This will be discussed in more detail later in the chapter.

Bernard Ramm (1916–1992), a very influential apologist of the latter part of the 20th century, also ignored the plain language of the creation account by advocating an illogical and dangerous approach to its interpretation. He stated, "No interpretation of Genesis 1 is more mature than the science that guides it."[4] In context, Ramm was referring to the fact that hermeneutics is a science. As such, one can only be as sure of his interpretation as he is of his science of interpretation. We do not take issue with this aspect of his comment. However, there are two major problems with his reasoning. The first problem lies in the fact that it is inconsistent to reserve this assertion to the Genesis

---

1. A. Berkeley Mickelsen, *Interpreting the Bible* (Grand Rapids, MI: Wm. B. Eerdmans, 1963), p. 306.
2. Ibid.
3. See Appendix C for an examination of the genealogies.
4. Bernard Ramm, *Protestant Biblical Interpretation* (Grand Rapids, MI: Baker Book House, 1970), p. 213.

text alone. After all, if somebody applies the same dictum to the resurrection of Jesus Christ, he will find that these accounts must refer to something other than a bodily resurrection. This is because the majority of scientists would say that resurrections are impossible. If proper interpretation of biblical texts depends on the approval of modern scientific opinion (as Ramm taught with regard to Genesis 1–11), then interpretation with any degree of certainty becomes impossible.

The second problem is that Ramm confessed that scientific philosophy based on numerous assumptions about the past should carry great weight in one's exegesis when he wrote:

> If uniformitarianism makes a scientific case for itself to a Christian scholar, that Christian scholar has every right to believe it, and if he is a man and not a coward he will believe it in spite of the intimidation that he is supposedly gone over into the camp of the enemy.[5]

This startling admission illustrates the dangerous hermeneutic Ramm endorsed. That is, if scientific opinion contradicts a person's understanding of God's Word, then he must change his interpretation of Scripture rather than question the scientific majority. One of the greatest problems with this approach is that scientific theories about the past are developed by fallible people who were not around to observe the events they are trying to study. Meanwhile, God's Word is inspired by the One who is infallible and is responsible for (and was an eyewitness to) the events that are being researched. In addition, scientific views are continually changing. During Ramm's lifetime, the scientific establishment's view on the age of the earth and the universe changed several times. Should Scripture be reinterpreted every time this occurs?

Old-earthers do not reject the ability of God to miraculously intervene in His creation, but they seem more than willing to agree with those who do reject this divine action. It is sad to see how such a great Christian man could side with the scoffers who mock the works of our Lord. The apostle Peter wrote of these people long before the

---

5. Bernard Ramm, *The Christian View of Science and Scripture* (Grand Rapids, MI: Wm. B. Eerdmans Publishers, 1954), p. 171.

debate over the age of the earth hit the scene. In his second letter, he wrote:

> Knowing this first of all, that scoffers will come in the last days with scoffing, following their own sinful desires. They will say, "Where is the promise of his coming? For ever since the fathers fell asleep, all things are continuing as they were from the beginning of creation." For they deliberately overlook this fact, that the heavens existed long ago, and the earth was formed out of water and through water by the word of God, and that by means of these the world that then existed was deluged with water and perished (2 Pet. 3:3–6; ESV).

Peter revealed that these scoffers would reject three important doctrines of the faith. First, they would reject the second coming of Jesus Christ ("Where is the promise of His coming?"). Second, they would willfully forget that "the earth was formed out of water and through water" by His Word. Third, they reject the fact that the original creation was destroyed by the Flood.

Perhaps even more important than these points is the philosophy that undergirds these beliefs. These scoffers believe that "all things continue as they were since the beginning of creation." This is uniformitarianism — the very belief that Ramm endorsed and said Christians can and should accept. Uniformitarianism simply states that the present is the key to the past. The uniformitarian geologist would claim that the current geologic processes that we observe today are normative for all history. For example, if it takes one hundred years to deposit a one-inch layer of sediment, then this must have always been the rate of deposition. Modern subscribers to uniformitarianism allow for local catastrophes throughout history to explain some of the earth's observable features. Nevertheless, according to their view, the majority of earth's features can only be explained by slow and gradual processes over millions of years.

The great Princeton theologian Charles Hodge (1797–1878) had adopted this view long before Ramm. In his *Systematic Theology*, Hodge promoted the day-age theory as a viable interpretation of Genesis 1. He wrote:

It is of course admitted that, taking this account by itself, it would be most natural to understand the word [day] in its ordinary sense; but if that sense brings the Mosaic account into conflict with facts, and another sense avoids such conflict, then it is obligatory on us to adopt that other [long periods of time].[6]

Here, Hodge encouraged Bible students to ignore the exegetically established interpretation of the text, if that interpretation caused a conflict with scientific "fact." Again, the problem is that the scientific "facts" promoted by Hodge have changed over the years since that statement, while the Bible has remained the same. As a result, when one adopts this hermeneutic, the meaning of God's Word must change whenever scientific opinion changes. Certainly, this is an unacceptable approach to the Word of the One whose words will never pass away (Matt. 24:35).

Another argument used by some evangelicals seems to be growing in popularity. It's called the "That's not the point of the passage!" argument. Some have suggested that it is not a big deal whether God created in six days or over millions of years because that is not the point of the passage. In this view, Genesis 1 is designed to teach us that God created and that man is unique in that he is created in God's image. The rest of the details are not worth debating because they are not part of the main point.

We might be willing to agree with these people that these are the two most important points in the creation account. However, this does not mean that the rest of the details are unimportant or inaccurate. First, if this view is correct, then why did the Holy Spirit inspire Moses to include the words of Genesis 1:2–25? Verse one tells us that God created everything and verses 26–31 deal with the creation of man. If the rest of the chapter is insignificant, why is it even part of the record?

The second problem with this view is that one cannot hold it consistently. For example, the apostle John reveals in his Gospel that he wrote it so that the reader might believe that Jesus is the Son of God and that by believing in Him "you may have life in His name"

---

6. Charles Hodge, *Systematic Theology*, originally published 1872 (Oak Harbor, WA: Logos Research Systems, Inc., 1997), p. 570–571.

(John 20:31). Certainly, this is the most important point in the book. That's why John wrote it! Does that mean that some of the details are unimportant? Does it really matter if all of the details concerning Christ's arrest in the Garden of Gethsemane are accurate? For example, what if Peter really did not draw his sword and cut off Malchus' ear (John 18:10)? This detail is not germane to John's theme. After all, he did not even mention that Jesus miraculously healed the servant's ear as some of the other Gospel writers did. If John was simply embellishing the story here to make Peter look brave, then can we really trust the rest of his Gospel? The details are not irrelevant to the main point of the passage. On the contrary, the details *establish* the main point.

If some details of God's Word cannot be trusted, how can we trust the rest? If some aren't important, why did God put them in the Bible? Jesus pointed this out when talking with Nicodemus. He asked, "If I have told you earthly things and you do not believe, how will you believe if I tell you heavenly things?" Likewise, why should a person trust the "main point" of the passage if the minor details cannot be trusted?

The Framework Hypothesis

Like Mickelsen, some have argued that the first chapter of Genesis should not necessarily be considered as historical narrative. Instead, supporters of the framework hypothesis claim that Genesis 1 is simply a literary framework and should not be viewed as a strict chronological account of creation events. Meredith Kline (1922–2007) of Westminster Theological Seminary was one of the most prominent advocates of this approach. Kline stated his purpose for advocating this view in his paper's introductory paragraph:

> To *rebut the literalist interpretation* of the Genesis creation week propounded by the young-earth theorists is a central concern of this article. At the same time, the exegetical evidence adduced *also refutes the harmonistic day-age view.* The conclusion is that as far as the time frame is concerned, with respect to both the duration and sequence of events, the

scientist is left free of biblical constraints in hypothesizing about cosmic origins.[7]

Kline's intentions are clear. His goals were to rebut "young-earth theorists"[8] and to free the scientist from any biblical constraints when "hypothesizing about cosmic origins." One must wonder about Kline's motives here. He greatly dislikes the young-earth position, which he called "a deplorable disservice to the cause of biblical truth." Why is a careful examination of the details of the verbally inspired text a deplorable disservice to the Bible? Also, while he did address the text in his paper, his conclusion that the scientist is free from any biblical constraints made it clear that the text is virtually meaningless in terms of coming to a sound conclusion. If Kline is correct, why did God include Genesis 1–11 in His Word in the first place? Why didn't He tell us the key points in a few sentences and leave the details for scientists to figure out?

If you are having trouble comprehending the framework hypothesis, think of Aesop's *Fables*. These are mythical stories that contain important teachings. It does not matter whether the tortoise ever raced the hare. What matters is that the reader understands the moral of the story — patience pays off.

One of Kline's former students, John Rankin, wrote at length concerning the framework hypothesis. While arguing against the young-earth creationist position, he wrote:

> It is well-intentioned, but with it comes an eisegetical import that the defense of the Bible against macroevolution requires the belief in a young universe and a young earth. Here, a view of a young universe and young planet is presuppositionally in place, and a wrong understanding of the Hebrew word *yom* explains it.[9]

---

7. Meredith Kline, "Space and Time in the Genesis Cosmogony," *Perspectives on Science and Christian Faith* 48:2 (1996), italics added for emphasis. Also available at http://www.asa3.org/ASA/PSCF/1996/PSCF3-96Kline.html. Accessed May 1, 2007.

8. Ibid.

9. John Rankin, p. 625. All quotations from Rankin come from personal correspondence with Bodie Hodge on 11/14/06. They are from a chapter that he wrote in a yet-to-be published book. Page numbers are based on that correspondence.

Notice Rankin accuses young-earth creationists of importing their young-earth beliefs into the Scripture. But the young-earther developed his idea of a young earth from Scripture. It seems that everyone, other than the framework followers, would accept that the young-earth creationists' view comes from Scripture or at the very least, a misinterpretation of Scripture. Yet, here young-earthers are charged with importing this belief into the text. Rankin claims that this view is based on a "wrong understanding of the Hebrew word *yom*." This particular argument will be covered later in this chapter.

Although framework proponents do not agree on every aspect, all of their views are heavily dependent upon the claim that Genesis 1 was written in poetic language. For example, Rankin stated, "The framework theory begins in recognition of the basic nature of Hebrew poetry, and its service to literary device."[10] Just what is the "basic nature of Hebrew poetry"? Rankin rightly explains, "Hebrew poetry is based on the concept of 'parallelism' of thought. . . . The idea of parallelism is to express an idea once, then to mirror or expand upon it in parallel or synonymous language."

Since they are poetic in nature, the Books of Psalms and Proverbs are full of parallelism. Psalm 49:1 provides a good example of the parallel nature of Hebrew poetry. "Hear this, all you peoples; listen, all who live in this world." The two lines of this couplet say essentially the same thing. Rankin correctly defines and illustrates this principle but then makes an unwarranted jump when interpreting Genesis 1. He wrote:

> In Genesis 1, all but v. 27 is written in prose, but the overall structure and details abound in the parallelisms of Hebrew poetry. It is in many ways the song of God's creation. The framework theory highlights this:
>
> Day 1 is parallel to Day 4;
> Day 2 is parallel to Day 5; and
> Day 3 is parallel to Day 6.[11]

---

10. Rankin, p. 630.
11. Ibid., p. 632.

There are a few problems with this argument. First, Rankin overstates the case regarding the similarities between the days. It is true that the creatures of the sea were created on the fifth day, but the water was not created on the second day. It was already there on the first day. Genesis 1:2 states, "And the Spirit of God was hovering over the face of the waters." The second day saw the creation of the firmament or expanse when the waters were divided. Also, the sun, moon, and stars were placed in the firmament on day 4, but the firmament was made on day 2, not day 1.

Second, these examples do not fit the mold of Hebrew poetry as defined above. The hallmark of Hebrew poetry is one idea being conveyed in two consecutive lines. Proponents of the framework view attempt to apply this to general concepts that are separated by several verses. This argument proves too much. Read the following examples from Scripture and consider whether or not the repeated idea nullifies the historicity of the passages so that they should be classified as poetic.

- Abraham and his son Isaac both had barren wives (Gen. 15:2 / 25:21)

- Both eventually had children through God's intervention (Gen. 21:2 / 25:24)

- Both men lied to authorities regarding their wives (Gen. 20:2 / 26:7)

- Both men faced famine in the Promised Land (Gen. 12:10 / 26:1)

- Both men made a covenant with the Philistines (Gen. 21:22–34 / 26:26–33)[12]

All of these occurrences appear in the Book of Genesis. First Samuel 24 and 26 record two different times when Saul pursued David

---

12. These similarities were pointed out by Dr. Noel Weeks in his 1979 article "Problems in Methods of Interpretation" available at http://www.answersingenesis.org/creation/v2/i4/interpretation.asp. Accessed May 1, 2007.

and both times David was given an opportunity to kill Saul. David spared Saul's life on both occasions.

Surely we are not to look at these parallels and consider them to be merely literary devices and that therefore Genesis 12–26 is all poetry. Nor would anyone claim that we have wrongly interpreted these passages as history because of our preconceived notions. However, if the framework proponents are consistent in their hermeneutics, then they should consider these passages as poetic and not actual historical accounts. We doubt any of them do.

These examples show us that it is actually the framework proponent who is guilty of eisegesis. While they claim that their "reinterpretation" is based on the words of Scripture, in reality, the only reason they desire to "reinterpret" Genesis 1 is because they have accepted old-earth claims. We will deal with more arguments based on poetry near the end of this chapter.

Kline and the others are misguided in their attempts to re-label the genre of the Genesis text. Dr. Steven Boyd, a Hebrew professor at The Master's College, recently conducted a careful statistical analysis of the verbs used in narrative and poetic passages in Scripture. He found that certain Hebrew verb forms dominate passages that all scholars agree are historical narrative, but that those same verb forms are seldom used in recognized poetic passages. Boyd's statistical analysis confirmed that Genesis 1 is undoubtedly historical narrative. Dr. Don DeYoung summarized Boyd's findings:

> The distribution of finite verbs in Hebrew narrative writing differs distinctly from that used in poetry. Moreover, statistical analysis categorizes biblical texts as narrative or poetry to a high level of accuracy. Genesis 1:1–2:3 is determined to be narrative with a probability of virtually one [the highest]. There follow at least three major implications from this study. First, it is not statistically defensible to interpret Genesis 1:1–2:3 as poetry or metaphor. Second, since Genesis 1:1–2:3 clearly is narrative, it should be read as other Hebrew narratives are intended to be read. That is, the creation account describes actual events which carry an unmistakable

theological message. Third, when Genesis 1:1–2:3 is read as narrative, there is only one tenable view: God created everything during six literal days. This is surely the plain, direct intention of the text.[13]

Genesis Is Just a Polemic

Another argument that has been raised against the young-earth position attempts to redefine the Genesis account as nothing more than a polemic written against the surrounding idolatrous peoples. Conrad Hyers, former Professor of Comparative Mythology and the History of Religions at Gustavus Adolphus College, wrote:

> *Polemic — a refutation of the opinions or principles of another.*

> In the light of this historical context it becomes clearer what Genesis 1 is undertaking and accomplishing: a radical and sweeping affirmation of monotheism vis-à-vis polytheism, syncretism and idolatry. Each day of creation takes on two principal categories of divinity in the pantheons of the day, and declares that these are not gods at all, but creatures — creations of the one true God who is the only one, without a second or third. Each day dismisses an additional cluster of deities, arranged in a cosmological and symmetrical order.[14]

Rather than being a historical report of actual events in space and time, Hyers proposed that each of the days of creation was written to counter the deities of the Egyptians, Babylonians, and Assyrians. Hyers would be considered a theological liberal due to his acceptance

---

13. Dr. Don DeYoung, *Thousands . . . Not Billions* (Green Forest, AR: Master Books, 2005), p. 169. Boyd's own technical study can be viewed at <http://www.icr.org/index.php?module=articles&action=view&ID=24>. Accessed May 1, 2007.

14. Conrad Hyers, "What Genesis Is Really About" Originally published in *Reports of the National Center for Science Education* 18: 3. Available online at <http://www.ncseweb.org/resources/rncse_content/vol18/328_what_genesis_is_ireallyi__12_30_1899.asp>. Accessed May 1, 2007.

of the now defunct JEPD theory.[15] Nevertheless, the ideas he promoted are gaining popularity among evangelicals who would never accept the JEPD theory. For example, in 1998, Dr. Mark Futato advanced similar ideas when he published an article in the *Westminster Theological Journal*, although he claimed that Genesis 1 was a polemic against the Canaanite gods — especially Baal.[16]

Hyers' claims fail for several reasons. First, he placed the authorship of Genesis in the 5th century B.C., approximately a thousand years after the conservative date of authorship. Conservative scholars, both old-earth and young-earth, agree that Moses wrote the Pentateuch in the 15th century B.C. If Genesis were composed during the life of Moses, then Hyers' theory collapses. While they may have been well acquainted with Egyptian mythologies, the wilderness-wandering Jews (who had been in Egypt for 400 years and were going to Canaan) would not have been heavily influenced by the mythologies of Assyria and Babylon. Second, there is nothing in the text to indicate its alleged polemical nature, even though it most certainly could be used as a polemic due to its historicity. This leads to the third fatal problem with Hyers' view. It would be nonsensical to develop a polemic against pagan mythologies that is nothing more than mythology itself. The only effective polemic is one that is based on real history. After all, if Hyers is correct, then one is left to choose one myth over another. What would give a Jew (or later, a Christian) the right to claim that his

15. Also called the "documentary hypothesis," the JEPD theory was developed in the 18th and 19th centuries by liberal theologians who based their view on the evolutionary theory. This view says that the Pentateuch (Genesis–Deuteronomy) was not written by Moses since it was believed that writing developed after his time. Instead, the books were written by at least four separate authors long after the time of Moses (J = the Yahwist, E = the Elohimist, D = Deuteronomist, P = Priestly). This theory has been completely debunked by evangelical scholars for several reasons. For example, it has been well established that writing was in existence long before Moses' time. The Code of Hammurabi dates to three centuries *before* the Exodus. The textual arguments for the JEPD theory have also been shown to be fatally flawed.

16. Dr. Mark Futato, "Because It Had Rained: A Study of Gen. 2:5–7 With Implications for Gen. 2:4–25 and Gen. 1:1–2:3," *Westminster Theological Journal Volume 60* (Westminster Theological Seminary, 1998, 2002): p. 20–21. In this article, Dr. Futato promoted the framework hypothesis. He argued that so much of Genesis 2–3 has to do with rain and vegetation it should be viewed as a polemic against the storm god Baal.

myth is better than the Babylonian, Assyrian, Egyptian, or Canaanite mythologies?

Contextual Conflicts

Much of the debate often centers on the meaning of *yom*, the Hebrew word usually translated as "day." Old-earth creationists are quick to point out that this word can mean something other than an ordinary 24-hour day. Young-earthers agree with this fact but remind people that the context of Genesis 1 indicates that the days were ordinary days. In response to this argument, old-earthers have crafted a few popular but faulty arguments.

Norman Geisler illustrates this poor reasoning. While responding to young-earthers' arguments concerning the normal meaning of the word *day*, he wrote:

> It is true that most often the Hebrew word *yom* ("day") means "twenty-four hours." However, this is not definitive for its meaning in Genesis 1 for several reasons.
>
> First, the meaning of a term is not determined by majority vote, but by the context in which it is used. It is not important how many times it is used elsewhere, but how it is used here.
>
> Second, even in the creation story in Genesis 1–2, "day" (*yom*) is used of more than a twenty-four-hour period. Speaking of the whole six "days" of creation, Genesis 2:4 refers to it as "the day" (*yom*) when all things were created.
>
> Third, and finally, *yom* is elsewhere used of long periods of time, as in Psalm 90:4, which is cited in 2 Peter 3:8: "A day is like a thousand years."[17]

We certainly agree with Geisler's first two points. Majority vote does not determine the meaning of a word but one should examine how it is translated in different contexts. If a particular context demands one interpretation then that is how it should be interpreted. Genesis 2:4 is utilizing merism — a figure of speech in which some parts are

---

17. Norman Geisler, *Systematic Theology, Volume Two* (Minneapolis, MN: Bethany House, 2003), p. 639.

cited to indicate the whole. As such, it is legitimate to interpret this as referring to the entire creation week. Young-earth creationists agree that this as an example in which *yom* does refer to something other than a 24-hour period.

There are some problems with Geisler's reasoning. Despite his plea for sticking with context, his two examples are not part of the context. Although Genesis 2:4 is in the creation account, it is not part of the narrative reporting of the first six days, each of which is paired with an ordinal or cardinal number as well as the phrase "evening and morning."

Geisler again ignores his contextual plea by quoting 2 Peter 3:8. This strategy is extremely common but is completely unfounded. First, Geisler does not finish the quote, which actually states, ". . . that with the Lord one day is as a thousand years, and a thousand years as one day." If this is supposed to offer support for the old-earth creationist view, it is difficult to see how it can. For example, if this is a mathematical equation that proves the days were long periods of time, then one must include the second part of the verse. Then the equation would be 1 day = 1,000 years = 1 day. No old-earther believes the creation period was 6,000 years long and if he did, it would not help him harmonize Genesis with the billions of years of evolutionary geology and cosmology. This does not help the old-earth position at all. Second, this quote is found in a passage dealing with the future return of Christ. It is simply indicating that God is not bound by time. Although it may seem like a long time to man, God is not neglecting His promise. He will send Christ back on His timetable, not ours.

Second Peter 3:8 is actually a *simile* — a comparison of two *dissimilar* things that have some resemblance. In this case, a day is contrasted with a thousand years, both brief time units when compared to God's eternality. If a "day" really could be translated as "a thousand years," then the simile would be silly; we could paraphrase it as, ". . . with the Lord a thousand years is as a thousand years, and a thousand years is as a thousand years." This would be true but hardly profound or worth saying. It is because a day is so *different* from a thousand years that the simile is so powerful. It indicates that God is beyond time and He works according to His plans and schedule, not ours.

Returning to Genesis 1, there are several Hebrew time-words that could have been used instead of *yom*, if the author meant to convey the idea of long periods of time. Russell Grigg cites other Hebrew words that would have made much more sense than *yom* if the days were long periods of time. Appropriately, he asks:

> Why did God not use any of these words with reference to the creation days, seeing that He used them to describe other things? Clearly it was His intention that the creation days should be regarded as being normal earth-rotation days, and it was not His intention that any longer time–frames should be inferred. [18]

Grigg's point should not be overlooked. God's Word was not written so that only the elite could understand it. While there are certainly difficult concepts and passages, the majority of it is written in simple language so that even children can understand it. This is known as the perspicuity of Scripture. That being the case, why would God use the word *yom* (the only Hebrew word that means a literal day and in virtually all cases does mean this) if He were really referring to a long period of time? The God of truth should have used a word that would lead people to believe in long periods of time, if indeed the billions of years are true.

Walter Kaiser, respected Old Testament scholar and seminary president, promoted a rather novel interpretation of Genesis 1 during his recent TV debate on the *John Ankerberg Show* in 2006.[19] While stressing that "context is king" in determining the meaning of a word, he claimed that the first three days did not need to be interpreted as ordinary days because God did not invent 24-hour days until the fourth creative period.

18. Russell Grigg, "How Long Were the Days of Genesis 1? What Did God Intend Us to Understand from the Words He Used?" *Creation* 19:1 (December 1996): p. 23–25.
19. "The Great Debate" involved Dr. Jason Lisle and Ken Ham against Dr. Kaiser and Dr. Hugh Ross and aired in February and March of 2006. The DVDs of the 10-part debate with added critical commentary by Dr. Terry Mortenson are available at <http://www.answersingenesis.org/PublicStore/product/GREAT-DEBATE-on-Science-and-the-Bible-The,5013,263.aspx>.

My answer is that God had not yet created a twenty-four hour day. So too bad for Brown-Driver-Briggs and too bad for Koehler-Baumgartner. Because it specifically says, I mean, if we're going to stick with the Bible, God created days on the fourth day. So we've got three of these yoms, which are not of the twenty-four hours.[20]

Brown-Driver-Briggs and Koehler-Baumgartner are the two most respected Hebrew lexicons. Both state that the word "*yom*" in the first three days should be interpreted in the same way as it is in days 4 through 6. Kaiser's argument runs counter to the reasoning of the best Hebrew scholars in the world.

Moreover, his argument collapses for several other reasons. First, the Bible does not say that God invented 24-hour days on the fourth creative period. It says that on the fourth day, God made the sun, moon, and stars by which to mark days (Gen. 1:14–19). This does not mean that the first three "days" could not have been ordinary days. It simply means that they were marked by something else — the light that God made on the very first day.

Second, Kaiser is inconsistent. His argument is allegedly based on the context of Genesis 1, yet he does not accept that days 4 through 6 are ordinary days, either. He says that they "are possible candidates for twenty-four hours."[21] If God created 24-hour days on the fourth day, why wouldn't the following days be ordinary days? Obviously, it is because Kaiser accepts the evolutionary geologists' and cosmologists' claims about the age of the earth and universe. Kaiser's view that days 4–6 could be literal days also contradicts the views of his debate partner, Hugh Ross, who argues that days 4, 5, and 6 are "literal, long periods of time."[22] Third, since he accepts the standard old-earth views regarding science, this forces numerous contradictions concerning the order of events put forth in Genesis 1.[23]

Fourth, Kaiser provides no explanation as to why the first three days are spoken of in the same manner as the next three days. Each day

20. *The Great Debate*, program 1.
21. Ibid.
22. Ibid.
23. See Appendix B for more information.

is mentioned with the phrase "evening and morning" and includes a cardinal or ordinal number. Also, as mentioned before, Exodus 20:11 groups all six days together and treats them as ordinary days (cf. Exod. 31:17–18). Why is no distinction made between these days, if Kaiser is correct that the context implies it? Obviously, it is because Kaiser's view is not consistent with Scripture but was simply created to allow him to accept the old-earth view. Sadly, this is another example of a futile effort of a brilliant Christian man to insert long ages into a biblical account that does not allow for them.

Creation of Adam and Eve

As stated in chapter 2, young-earth creationists often cite Jesus' statements on marriage as solid evidence in support of their view. Both Matthew and Mark record Jesus' exchange with the Pharisees. When questioned about marriage and divorce, Jesus replied, "Have you not read that He who made them at the beginning 'made them male and female . . .' " (Matt. 19:4). Very few old-earthers have even commented on this young-earth argument, much less refuted it.[24]

In his popular systematic theology, Wayne Grudem is undecided about the age of the earth, but clearly leans toward the old-earth view. He offered a possible old-earth creationist's response to this argument.

> [The young-earth creationist's] argument also has some force, but old earth advocates may respond that Jesus is just referring to the whole of Genesis 1–2 as the "beginning of creation," in contrast to the argument from the laws given by Moses that the Pharisees were depending on.[25]

This interpretation is certainly not the natural reading of the text, since Jesus said that male and female were created "at the beginning." For Jesus to say only a few thousand years after Adam that the first 10–20 billion years were "the beginning" would be like calling January 1 through December 31 11:59:51 P.M. the "beginning of the year."

---

24. For a detailed analysis on this point, see Terry Mortenson, "Jesus, Evangelical Scholars and the Age of the Earth," *The Master's Seminary Journal,* vol. 18 (1) (Spring 2007): p. 69–98.
25. Wayne Grudem, *Systematic Theology* (Grand Rapids, MI: Zondervan, 1994), p. 297.

Norman Geisler also addressed this argument but focused on Mark's recording of the conversation. Mark wrote, "But from the beginning of the creation, God made them male and female" (Mark 10:6). Geisler offered three arguments to refute the young-earth position.

First, Adam was not created at the beginning but at the end of the creation period (on the sixth day), no matter how long or short the days were.

Second, the Greek word for "create" (*ktisis*) can and sometimes does mean "institution" or "ordinance" (cf. 1 Peter 2:13). Since Jesus is speaking of the institution of marriage in Mark 10:6, it could mean "from the beginning of the institution of marriage."

Third, and finally, even if Mark 10:6 is speaking of the original creation events, it does not mean there could not have been a long period of time involved in those creative events.[26]

These arguments will be discussed in the order presented. In the first argument, Geisler attempts to show that Adam and Eve were not made "at the beginning," no matter what view one holds. After all, Adam and Eve were made on the sixth day, which is at the end of the creation week. Geisler implies that Jesus was wrong if He was saying that man was made "at the beginning" of history. Since Jesus, being God, cannot make a mistake, then this must be the wrong interpretation. It is important to notice that Geisler added the word "period" to the text. Jesus simply said that it was "from the beginning of the creation" not "from the beginning of the creation period." Jesus was talking about all of creation from His day back to the beginning of creation.

It is certainly reasonable that the very first week would count as the "beginning of creation" even though Adam and Eve were made near the end of that week. For example, consider a marathon runner who stumbles about 20 feet into the race. When asked for his thoughts about his performance during the race, he could respond, "Well, I did pretty good, except I stumbled *at the beginning* of the race." No one would accuse the runner of being inaccurate even though, technically, he did not stumble in his first step.

26. Geisler, *Systematic Theology, Vol. 2*, (2003), p. 642.

It seems that Geisler probably opts for the second argument in which he claims Jesus was simply referring to the "creation" or "institution" of marriage. He used these same arguments while writing an article with Dr. John Ankerberg.[27] In response to their claims, Dr. Terry Mortenson wrote:

> [Ankerberg and Geisler] argue that *ktisis* (which is actually the noun "creation" not the verb "create," as A/G say) in Mark 10:6 should be translated as "institution" so that Jesus should be understood to be talking about the beginning of the institution of marriage, not the beginning of creation. They base this interpretation on the fact that in 1 Pet 2:13 *ktisis* is translated in the NIV as "to every authority instituted among men" or in the NASB as "to every human institution." But they have not paid careful attention to the presence of "among men" (NIV) and "human" (NASB) in this verse.
>
> The Greek text is clear. The phrase under question is *pasē anthrōpinē ktisei*, where the whole phrase is in the dative case (so literally "to every human creation") and the adjective *anthrōpinē* ("human") modifies *ktisei* ("creation"). An institutional authority (such as kings, governors and slave masters, which Peter discusses in the context) is indeed a "human creation." But this is a very different contextual use of *ktisis* than we find in Mark 10:6, where no adjective is used to modify "creation." Furthermore, in Mark 10:6 Jesus could have easily said "from the first marriage" or "from the beginning of marriage" or "since God created man" or "since God created Adam," if that is what He meant.
>
> Finally, if we give *ktisis* in Mark 10:6 the meaning "authority" or "institution," it makes no sense. What does from the beginning of authority or beginning of institution mean? To make it meaningful Ankerberg and Geisler would have to add a word to the text, which would have no contextual justification.

---

27. John Ankerberg and Norman Geisler, "Differing Views of the 'Days' of Genesis." <http://www.johnankerberg.com/Articles/science/SC0704W1.htm> Accessed May 1, 2007.

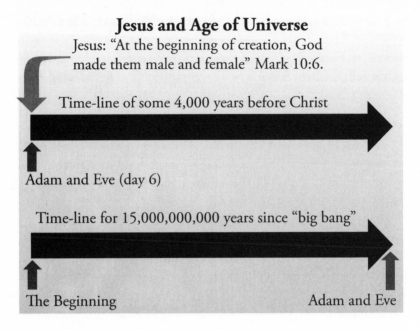

Jesus and Age of Universe

Jesus: "At the beginning of creation, God made them male and female" Mark 10:6.

Time-line of some 4,000 years before Christ

Adam and Eve (day 6)

Time-line for 15,000,000,000 years since "big bang"

The Beginning   Adam and Eve

Jesus is reaching farther back in history for the basis of his teaching on marriage. The Pharisees go back to the time of Moses' writings in Deuteronomy, whereas Jesus goes back to the beginning of time. Jesus spoke these words about 4,000 years after the beginning. If we equate those 4,000 years with a 24-hour day, then Jesus was speaking at 24:00 and the creation of Adam and Eve on the sixth literal day of history would be equivalent to 00:00:00:35 (half a second after the beginning), in the non-technical language of Jesus here is the beginning of time. So, Jesus is indeed saying that Adam and Eve were at the beginning of creation.[28]

Finally, Geisler's third argument is also fatally flawed. If Matthew and Mark were "speaking of the original creation events," it absolutely means there could not have been a long period of time involved in those creative events. For example, even if hundreds of years elapsed before Adam and Eve were created, there is no possible way for Jesus

---

28. Terry Mortenson, "But from the Beginning of . . . the Institution of Marriage," <http://www.answersingenesis.org/docs2004/1101ankerberg_response.asp> Accessed May 1, 2007.

to be correct in His assertion that God made Adam and Eve "at the beginning." Notice that this becomes a major problem when one adds hundreds of years. How much more severe is the problem if the desired billions of years are added?

The Length of the Seventh Day

Another argument that is commonly used to suggest that the first six days could have been longer than ordinary days is summarized by Geisler:

> Everyone agrees that it has been at least thousands of years since the time of creation, yet the Bible declares that God rested on the seventh day after His six days of creation (Gen. 2:2–3). According to the book of Hebrews, God is still in His Sabbath rest from creation (4:3–5); hence, the seventh day has been at least six thousand years long, even on the shortest of all the chronologies of humankind.[29]

Although his logic is typically very sound, it escapes Geisler here. Hebrews 4:3–5 actually states:

> For we who have believed do enter that rest, as He has said: "So I swore in My wrath, 'They shall not enter My rest,' " although the works were finished from the foundation of the world. For He has spoken in a certain place of the seventh day in this way: "And God rested on the seventh day from all His works"; and again in this place: "They shall not enter My rest."

First, notice that the text does not say that the seventh day of the creation week is continuing to the present day. It merely reveals that God entered His rest on the seventh day. An illustration may be helpful here. Imagine that a vacationing person said on Monday that he rested on Friday. It would not be reasonable to suggest that, since he was still resting on Monday, therefore it was still Friday. Second, this popular old-earth argument creates a theological problem as well. John Whitcomb illustrated this problem over 30 years ago:

---

29. Geisler, *Systematic Theology, Vol. 2*, (2003), p. 643.

We must assume that the seventh day was a literal day because Adam and Eve lived through it before God drove them out of the Garden. Surely, he would not have cursed the earth during the seventh day which he blessed and sanctified (Gen. 2:1–3; Exod. 31:12–17).[30]

Old-earth creationists also bring up the fact that the seventh day does not contain the familiar "evening and morning" phrase. As such, they say, the seventh day must be a long period of time, in accordance with their interpretation of Hebrews 4:3–5. If the seventh day can be a longer period of time, then surely the first six days could be as well. This argument actually proves too much. If the exclusion of the phrase "evening and morning" allows the seventh day to be longer, then this is really an unintentional admission that the first six days were literal 24-hour days.

Finally, one should not press the idea of God's rest from His creative works too far. The author of Hebrews used it as an analogy of the spiritual rest offered to those who trust in Christ. Also, to believe that God is still resting in an absolute sense would run contrary to many of the miraculous events in Scripture. Some of these miracles involved the creative works such as the Lord's feeding of the five thousand (Matt. 14:21) and the four thousand (Matt. 15:34–38). Jesus declared, "My Father has been working until now, and I have been working" (John 5:17). God is still working; He's just no longer creating the universe. This is the *rest* described in Genesis 2:2. Today, God is working by upholding and sustaining the universe He made (Heb. 1:3; Col. 1:17).

Poetic Considerations

It has become popular lately for old-earthers to try and use poetic sections of the Bible to override the plain teachings of historical sections. Since a straightforward reading of Genesis does not support their view, some old-earth creationists hope to reinforce their position by selectively quoting poetic passages like Psalms or Proverbs. Hugh Ross states:

---

30. John C. Whitcomb Jr., "The Science of Historical Geology," *Westminster Theological Journal*, Volume 36 (1974): p. 68.

. . . not all the answers are in Genesis. And in particular, there's three of them: Proverbs 8, Psalm 104, and Job 38 and 39 that actually take you through each of the six creation days of Genesis 1. And when you do that (integrate those four in particular) you discover that it's not possible to take that word "yom" in any context other than a long period of time.[31]

But, when read in context, there is nothing in these poetic sections of Scripture that would contradict a straightforward reading of Genesis: that God did indeed create in six literal days. After all, the same God that inspired Genesis also inspired these sections of the Bible. But since poetic books, like the Psalms, Proverbs, and Job, contain figures of speech, metaphors, and other non-literal imagery, many people feel a greater liberty to interpret these passages as they wish, rather than according to the standard rules of biblical interpretation. Some old-earth creationists have even mislabeled poetic passages as "accounts of creation," presumably in an attempt to revise the biblical history by pulling certain poetic sections out of context.

In one of his more recent books, Hugh Ross lists 21 "major creation accounts in the Bible."[32] Many of the passages are from poetic sections of the Bible; four of the listed passages are from the Psalms, two are from Job.[33] Proverbs and Ecclesiastes are also included. Sections of the Bible such as the Psalms are not "accounts" at all, but rather poetic songs of praise to God. They are just as inspired and true as the rest of God's Word; however, they require knowledge of the historic narrative sections of the Bible in order to fully understand and properly interpret the poetic language.

One of the most important rules of hermeneutics is that the unclear should be interpreted in light of the clear; therefore, poetic sections using symbolism and literary imagery should be interpreted in light of the more straightforward historical narratives. This is not

---

31. "Heart and Soul" BBC radio broadcast. (Hugh Ross is interviewed by Eugenie Scott.) Accessed March 30, 2007. 19:46–20:12.
   <http://www.bbc.co.uk/worldservice/programmes/heart_and_soul.shtml>.
   Accessed 3/30/2007.
32. Hugh Ross, *A Matter of Days* (Colorado Springs, CO: NavPress, 2004), p. 66.
33. For that matter, many of the narrative passages Ross cites do not pertain to the initial creation at all, such as Genesis 6–9; these verses describe the Flood.

to say that poetic sections never shed light on narratives; they can. But they should never be used to override the clear teaching of historical narratives. Consider Exodus 14–15. Chapter 14 is written in historical narrative style; this chapter contains the account of the parting of the Red Sea. Chapter 15 is poetic; it contains a song that the Israelites sang commemorating this event. The events of chapter 14 allow us to understand the song in chapter 15.

However, it would be silly to take the poetic descriptions of chapter 15 in a woodenly literal sense and then reinterpret chapter 14 accordingly. The inhabitants of Canaan did not literally "melt away" (verse 15). The Egyptians were not literally "burned" or "consumed" (verse 7), they were drowned. Imagine if we used this symbolic imagery to suggest that God actually destroyed the Egyptians by fire — not water. Imagine that we "reinterpreted" chapter 14 to accommodate such a notion. This would be a pretty obvious mistake in hermeneutics.

Yet, errors of this kind are common in old-earth theology. Old-earth creationist Tim Boyle uses Psalm 104 in an attempt to override the clear teaching of Genesis that the original animals were vegetarian. He writes, "Psalm 104 praises God for his initial good creation, in all its aspects. Beginning with verse 21, it speaks of God's creation of animals — both herbivorous and carnivorous."[34] However, verse 21 says nothing about the creation of the original animals; it only mentions that lions roar after their prey. Since Genesis 1:29–30 clearly teaches that animals were originally to eat plants alone, Psalm 104:21 cannot be referring to the way things were originally, but rather the way things are at the time the psalm was written, about 3,000 years after Adam's sin and God's curse on the creation.

It really should be obvious from the other verses of Psalm 104 that this passage is not an account of creation. Verse 16 refers to the "cedars of Lebanon." Are we to believe that the nation of Lebanon existed during the creation week? Verse 26 mentions "ships." Are we to believe that God created the oceans with ships sailing on them? The psalm also mentions wine and oil (v. 15), which are man-made, and clouds and lightning (vv. 3–4), which are not mentioned in Genesis

---

34. T. Boyle, *Reasons to Believe* newsletter, May 2005, p. 6

1. Clearly these verses of Psalm 104 are speaking of the present world, not the original paradise. Although some verses of Psalm 104 touch on creation, the chapter is clearly not an *account* of creation, but a praise of how God cares over His works. In today's fallen world, God provides meat for carnivores, but in the beginning it was not so.

The Ancient Hills

The important principle of interpreting the unclear in light of the clear extends to all portions of Scripture. Another area in which this principle is violated concerns the old-earthers' claim that certain biblical passages *explicitly* teach that the earth is old. Hugh Ross and Gleason Archer state:

> Habakkuk 3:6 directly declares that the mountains are "ancient" and the hills are "age-old." In 2 Peter 3:5, Peter tells us that the heavens (the stars and the universe) existed "long ago." Such descriptions of certain aspects of creation would have little impact if the earth and its hills were literally only a few days older than humankind. The point of contrast would be lost.[35]

Once again, we see a poetic passage in Habakkuk used to override the clear teaching in Genesis. We see the general statement in 2 Peter that the heavens existed "long ago" used to override the clear teaching of Genesis that tells us specifically how long ago. The proper hermeneutic is to evaluate these generalities in light of the clear specifics. In other words, the above verses tell us the hills are old, but not specifically how old. It is the historical narratives that provide us with that specific information and tell us how to interpret more vague statements of Habakkuk and 2 Peter.

The above verses are perfectly consistent with a literal reading of Genesis. The hills *are* old — thousand of years old! The biblical passages in no way suggest that the world is *billions* of years old. The Hebrew word for "age-old" used in Habakkuk is "olam" (עולם). This word does imply age, but not necessarily billions of years. After all,

---

35. David G. Hagopian, ed., *The Genesis Debate* (Mission Viejo, CA: CruX Press, 2001), p. 147.

the same word is used to describe *people* in Genesis 6:4 — the "men of old." These men might have been very old,[36] but not billions of years old. Clearly, the biblical statements that the hills are age-old and that the heavens existed long ago do not support the notion of a multi-billion-year-old earth and universe.

---

36. Genesis 6 describes the pre-Flood world. At that time, many people lived to be several hundred years old, according to the genealogies listed in Genesis 5.

Chapter 4

Defense — Poor Reasoning

T he previous chapter looked at some of the attempts made by old-earthers to respond to young-earth biblical arguments. The defense and cross-examination will continue in this chapter. This time we will direct our attention to their theological arguments.

Pragmatic Appeals

Pragmatism is the belief that whatever "works" must be right or true. Perhaps the most erroneous argument used by some old-earthers is that young-earth creationism is actually a hindrance to the work of evangelism. Hugh Ross wrote, "As circumcision distorted the gospel and hampered evangelism, so, too, does young-earth creationism."[1] No doubt, the lost have been reached through the work of old-earthers, including Hugh Ross. However, young-earth creationism does not distort the gospel but clearly affirms it. There is a subtle implication of this old-earth accusation that is also false: young-earth creationists do not say that a person has to accept a young earth to be saved. But also, many people have written to AiG and other creationist ministries to say that they came to faith in Christ precisely because of the young-earth creationist literature or videos. In any case, ultimately it is the Holy Spirit that convicts of sin, and enables us to say that Jesus is Lord.[2]

1. Dr. Hugh Ross, *Creation and Time* (Colorado Springs, CO: NavPress, 1994), p. 162.
2. 1 Corinthians 12:3

Additionally, the effectiveness of a technique should not be used as a test of its truthfulness. We could probably produce "converts" (in name at least) by promising vast earthly wealth, perfect health, and continual earthly happiness for all those who trust in Jesus; but such a method would be dishonest. The ends do not justify the means.

Dr. Robert Pyne of Dallas Theological Seminary has put forth another pragmatic argument. He believes that we need to come up with a better strategy to reach the lost who have bought into the idea of evolution. In the seminary's latest work on systematic theology, Pyne likened the creation-evolution debate to a ballgame. He claims that the problem for creationists is that the rules of the game only allow for naturalistic explanations of the world's origin. As such, we must be disqualified, but we refuse to exit the field. Pyne writes:

> From that vantage point [the seats] we can see that those [young-earthers] who still try to play the game are failing, but they have convinced themselves they are succeeding. We call attention to their failure, but only to criticize the futility of the game itself.[3]

Contrary to Pyne's statement, the game is not futile, especially in light of the fact that God has used the efforts of creationist ministries to save thousands of individuals. Unfortunately, Pyne has been caught up in the movement that seeks to legitimize some form of old-earth creationism by gaining acceptance among secular academia. Pyne wrote, "However, I, too, would prefer to see contemporary discussions turn to the more winnable (and more significant) issue of intelligent design."[4] God has not commanded His people to play the game by the world's standards. He has called His people to proclaim His Word because it is what will accomplish His purposes (Isa. 55: 11).[5]

The issue of intelligent design may be "more winnable" according to the rules of Pyne's naturalistic game, but it is certainly not "more

---

3. Charles Swindoll and Roy B. Zuck, eds., *Understanding Christian Theology* (Nashville, TN: Thomas Nelson Publishers, 2003), p. 657.
4. Ibid., p. 671.
5. See Appendix D for more on Intelligent Design.

significant." More than one billion Muslims (as well as thousands of other non-Christians in the ID movement itself) believe in intelligent design but are still lost because they do not know the Intelligent Designer who has revealed himself in His Word. The reason we are involved in the creation vs. evolution debate is not just to teach people to believe in the existence of a vaguely defined creator but to show them that they need to place their faith in *the* Creator to save them from their sins.

Actually, the debate between old-earth creationists and young-earth creationists is not really about the age of the earth and universe. Primarily, it comes down to biblical authority. Did God really do what He said He did in Genesis 1? If it took Him billions of years to create everything, then He could have easily and clearly stated that in His Word.

"Creation Agnosticism"

Dr. Pyne concluded his chapter by stating that dinosaurs probably lived "a long, long time ago" and that "it looks like they all died before any people got to see them."[6] He continues, "Some of our friends [young-earth creationists] think people did see them [dinosaurs], and they may turn out to be right."[7] This statement reveals another approach used by some theologians who favor the old-earth view, and this approach seems to be gaining acceptance among conservative scholars. Briefly stated, their position is that the Bible does not give enough information about the age of the earth so one really cannot base his conclusions on Scripture. Instead, one should look to science to answer such questions.

In his *Systematic Theology*, Wayne Grudem advocates the idea that one cannot really know:

> Therefore, with respect to the length of days in Genesis 1, the possibility must be left open that God has chosen not to give us enough information to come to a clear decision on this question, and the real test of faithfulness to him may be the degree to which we can act charitably toward those who in

---

6. Swindoll and Zuck, eds., *Understanding Christian Theology*, p. 671.
7. Ibid.

good conscience and full belief in God's Word hold to a different position on this matter.[8]

Grudem's second point is appropriate and echoes the purpose of this book. True debate can only occur when sound arguments are utilized in a civil manner. However, it is Grudem's first point that must be scrutinized. Nothing in the text of Genesis 1 or any other place in Scripture, for that matter, would indicate an age of the earth beyond several thousand years. Grudem recognized the considerable strength of the young-earth creationist's theological position:

> At present, considerations of the power of God's creative word and the immediacy with which it seems to bring response, the fact that "evening and morning" and the numbering of days still suggest twenty-four-hour days, and the fact that God would seem to have no purpose for delaying the creation of man for thousands or even millions of years seem to me to be strong considerations in favor of the twenty-four-hour day position.[9]

Nevertheless, after a balanced discussion of the issue, he does not take a stand. Instead, he cites 2 Peter 3:8 to demonstrate God's eternality and reasons that the "evidence of incredible antiquity in the universe would then serve as a vivid reminder of the even more amazing nature of God's eternity. . . ."[10]

In his influential *Genesis in Space and Time*, popular Christian philosopher Francis Schaeffer also sought to avoid the debate by pleading "creation agnosticism." After listing three possible interpretations of *yom*, Schaeffer concluded:

> Therefore, we must leave open the exact length of time indicated by day in Genesis. From the study of the word in Hebrew, it is not clear which way it is to be taken; it could be either way. In the light of the word as used in the Bible and the

---

8. Wayne Grudem, *Systematic Theology* (Grand Rapids, MI: Zondervan, 1994), p. 297.
9. Ibid.
10. Ibid.

lack of finality of science concerning the problem of dating, in a sense there is no debate, because there are no clearly defined terms upon which to debate.[11]

But Schaeffer fails to give any analysis of the use of *yom* or deal with creationist biblical arguments for literal days and a young earth (though such arguments were in print when Schaeffer wrote).

Christian apologist and philosopher J.P. Moreland has used this tactic as well. On at least two occasions, Moreland stated, "I'm an old-earth creationist five days out of the week; I'm a young-earth creationist two days out of the week."[12] The statement itself is intriguing. One is tempted to ask, "Do you mean five ordinary days, or five long periods of time — perhaps millions of years each?" Of course we understand him to mean ordinary days because of the context. Likewise, we know the days of Genesis 1 are ordinary days because of the context, and therefore the earth is young.

But why does Moreland waffle so much on this issue? Could it be that he truly believes the Bible teaches a young earth but cannot bring himself to believe it because of scientific opinion? Apparently, this is precisely the reason. During a lecture at Northshore Church in Everett, Washington, on February 2, 2002, Moreland demonstrated an acceptance of secular scientific opinion. Also, Moreland refused to address the biblical arguments for a young earth. Instead, he appealed to authority when he cited fellow old-earthers Walter Kaiser and Gleason Archer.[13]

Misrepresenting the Other Side

Moreland's comments at Northshore Church promote some other poor old-earth arguments. In an effort to repudiate the young-earth

11. Francis Schaeffer, *The Complete Words of Francis A. Shaeffer: Genesis in Space and Time*, Vol. 2 (Westchester, IL: Crossway Books, 1982), p. 39.

12. Moreland at the Association of Christian Schools International convention, November 2000 in Denver, Colorado.

13. Moreland's comments are available at the Reasons to Believe website <http://www.reasons.org/resources/apologetics/moreland_jp_age_of_earth.shtml?main>. For a thorough critique of Moreland's arguments see: Ken Ham, Carl Wieland, and Terry Mortenson, "Are Biblical Creationists Cornered?" available at <http://www.answersingenesis.org/tj/v17/i3/creationists.asp>. Accessed May 1, 2007.

position, Moreland linked it to the myths that Scripture teaches geo-centricism and a flat earth.[14] This approach is typical from old-earth creationists and naturalistic evolutionists. Contrary to popular opinion, the Church as a whole never accepted the concept of a flat earth, and neither does Scripture teach it. In fact, the Bible reveals the earth is round in several places. Isaiah 40:22 states that God "sits above the circle of the earth." Job 26:10 poetically describes God inscribing a "circle on the surface of the waters at the boundary of light and darkness." This boundary between light and darkness is where evening and morning occur and is always a circle because the earth is spherical.

Moreland's linking of young-earth creationists with geocentri-cism is an example of guilt by association: it discredits young-earth creationism by associating it with a view that is widely rejected. It does not matter that many in the medieval Church held to a geocentric view. The Bible does not teach it. If any-thing, the medieval Church's acceptance of this view illustrates the danger of marrying the biblical text with scientific opinions of the time. Geocentricism was the view of the scientific community at the time. Supporters often used a hyper-literal reading of Joshua 10:12–13 to buttress their position. However, it is quite obvious that Joshua was simply using observational language. The same thing is commonly employed by trained meteorologists today when they speak of the sun "rising" and "setting." Surely, no one would accuse these men of believing that the earth is stationary and the sun revolves around it!

> *Geocentricism —*
> *the belief that the*
> *earth is at the center*
> *of the universe.*

Geocentricists would also cite poetic verses such as Psalm 96:10 to support their view. This verse says that the world "shall not be moved." However, the Hebrew word for "moved" (מוֹט, *môt*) does not necessarily imply motion in an absolute sense, but rather "to slip," or to be "out of course." In fact, David also says in Psalm 62:6, "I shall not be moved" using the same Hebrew word. Is David indicating that he will never physically move? Clearly not. He is indicating that he will not deviate from the path the Lord laid out for him. Likewise, the earth will not deviate from its path. Clearly, the Bible does not teach

---

14. Ibid.

geocentricism, and neither do we. But the Bible does teach a young earth.

Taking the lead from Bible skeptics and critics, some old-earthers introduce the infamous trial of Galileo in an effort to attack young-earth creationism. The Galileo affair is presented as a battle over religious interpretation and scientific fact. They proceed to claim that the Church's interpretation was wrong in the 17th century and needed to be adjusted according to the latest scientific findings. Similarly, they say, young-earth creationists hold a wrong interpretation of Scripture that needs to be conformed to the latest scientific views.[15]

First, the whole Galileo controversy has been distorted. It is true that most religious leaders of the day held to a geocentric view of the universe. Nevertheless, Galileo found himself in trouble with Rome because of his arrogance and harsh criticism of the pope, not because of his scientific views.[16] In fact, many Jesuit astronomers were open to Galileo's teachings. The Jesuit missionaries to China were teaching heliocentricity within 30 years of Galileo's discovery. It was actually the academicians of the day who rejected Galileo because of their acceptance of Aristotelian beliefs. They persuaded the Church to reject Galileo's claims. It is simply disingenuous to link young-earth creationism with the Church of Galileo's day.

Ironically, this popular attack on young-earth creationism actually backfires. The Roman Catholic Church is being accused of accepting the scientific views of the day. When new scientific evidence came along, they clung to their old views of science because they claimed scriptural support for their view. This is exactly what old-earthers do today. They cling to modern scientific theories and try to marry the Scriptures to them. These scientific opinions frequently change, and the old-earthers' beliefs just change right along with them.

Old-earthers try to make the connection between young-earth creationism and these two views because they wish to demonstrate that young-earth creationism is based on an over-literal interpretation of the

---

15. Craig Rusbult, PhD, "Age of the Earth: Why It Does and Doesn't Matter," <http://www.asa3.org/ASA/education/origins/whyoe.htm>. Accessed May 1, 2007.

16. Thomas Schirrmacher, "The Galileo Affair: History or Heroic Hagiography?" *TJ* 14:1 (April 2000): p. 91–100.

text. In fact, young-earthers are often called "literalists."[17] Once again, this argument fails. Young-earth creationists would generally accept being called "literalists" but not in the form that old-earthers misuse the term. What they typically refer to in this context would be more accurately called "letterism" or "wooden literalism." Letterism does not allow for the use of figurative or poetic language. Instead, every word is to be taken in a wooden literal sense. Young-earth creationists do not accept this hermeneutic; rather, we use the historical-grammatical approach, which acknowledges the various literary styles in Scripture and interprets them as such.[18] Unfortunately for the old-earth creationists, Genesis 1 is clearly historical narrative, not poetry, parable, prophetic vision, or some other figurative literature.

The popular old-earth creationist website *Answers in Creation* provides a classic example of what is known as a straw-man argument. A straw-man argument is a very common debating tactic. This occurs when one side wrongly defines or describes the opposing position in an inaccurate way to make it easy to defeat. After all, a straw man is much easier to knock down than a real man. When discussing the possibility of whether or not Job 40–41 is referring to dinosaurs, the writer makes the following absurd claim:

> When discussing this topic, young-earthers always go to the behemoth and leviathan of Job. However, these creatures don't fit the description of dinosaurs, using young-earth standards. Remember that young-earth creationists are literalists, and believe every verse of the Bible is to be taken literally. In that case, Leviathan must have actually breathed fire (Job 41). However, there are no known dinosaurs with this capability. For Behemoth, no dinosaur had bones of bronze or iron.[19]

Most young-earth creationists have no trouble believing that some kind of dinosaur or similar creature could have breathed fire. Since all

---

17. See Meredith Kline, "Space and Time in the Genesis Cosmogony," *Perspectives on Science and Christian Faith* 48:2 (1996): p. 2.

18. For an excellent summary of the young-earth hermeneutic, see Russell Grigg, "Should Genesis Be Taken Literally?" *Creation* 16:1 (Dec. 1993): p. 38–41.

19. <http://www.answersincreation.org/bookreview/answersbook/abc19.htm>. Accessed April 30, 2007.

we have are the bones of these creatures, it is impossible to rule out this prospect. But several living creatures strongly suggest that this is not a far-fetched idea: some eels produce electricity. Fireflies produce light and bombardier beetles produce an explosive, noxious gas heated to the boiling temperature of water. Also, no one believes these creatures had bones that were made of bronze. The Bible does not say this either. The text says that behemoth's "bones are like beams of bronze" and his "ribs like bars of iron." Obviously, the author is employing the figure of speech known as a simile. The text is simply revealing that this creature's bones were exceedingly strong because he was an enormous creature. Not only does the author of this article misrepresent the young-earth creationists' hermeneutic, he also misquotes the Bible to make his point.

Old-earthers often intentionally misrepresent the young-earth position. It is sometimes difficult to fairly represent the opposing view because every person has a bias. Nonetheless, every attempt should be made to truthfully present both sides of the debate. Many of the old-earthers quoted in the following section are notable evangelical scholars and should know better. The reason they misrepresent young-earthers is to make their view look better by comparison.

Young-earthers are often presented as hard-line fundamentalists who believe that all old-earthers are heretics who should be thrown out of the Church. This is simply not true. Ken Ham, the president of *Answers in Genesis*, wrote, "We do not seek to pass judgment on his Christian character or his commitment to the Lord." [20] This particular statement was made in reference to Hugh Ross, who is perhaps the most well-known old-earth creationist in the world.

Although we do not question the Christian commitment of the old-earther, young-earth creationists will often warn of what they see as a dangerous hermeneutical precedent. That is, if the days of the creation week can be interpreted as long periods of time, where does one stop reinterpreting Scripture on the basis of modern scientific opinions? For example, the majority of scientists do not believe that dead people can come back to life. If one applies the same hermeneutic to

20. <http://www.answersingenesis.org/docs/4077.asp>. Accessed May 1, 2007. See also Sarfati, *Refuting Compromise*, p. 26.

the resurrection of Jesus Christ, then he must conclude that Christ did not rise from the dead, which means our faith is futile (1 Cor. 15:17).

In 2000, Dr. John Ankerberg hosted a debate between Dr. Hugh Ross and Dr. Kent Hovind. As moderator, Ankerberg revealed his old-earth bias on numerous occasions by siding with Ross. Ankerberg stated, "The argument that *yom* never means anything in the Bible but a literal 24 hours is completely untenable in the light of scriptural usage elsewhere."[21] Ankerberg is absolutely correct that *yom* can mean something other than an ordinary day. The problem is that Dr. Hovind does not believe that *yom* never means anything but a literal day, as Ankerberg implied, and neither does any other informed young-earther. Ankerberg used a common attack on young-earth creationists by misrepresenting their position on the Hebrew word for "day."

In his *Systematic Theology,* Geisler offers an appendix on the "Various Views of the 'Days' of Genesis." Among his arguments for the young-earth view, Dr. Geisler offers the following straw-man argument:

> It is well known that the theory of evolution (or common ancestry) depends on very long periods of time for life to develop from a one-celled animal to human beings. Without these long periods of time, evolution would not be possible. Thus, it is argued by young-earthers that granting long periods of time is an accommodation to evolution.[22]

Dr. Geisler proceeds to torch this straw man by correctly pointing out, "scientists had concluded that long periods of time were involved before Darwin wrote in 1859."[23] Again, the problem with this argument is that no informed young-earth creationist claims that "long periods of time [are] an accommodation to evolution." Young-earthers agree with Geisler that the idea of an old-earth predates Darwin's writings. It would be accurate to claim that these "long periods of time" are an accommodation to uniformitarian geology popularized in the early 19th century by James Hutton and Charles Lyell. In fact, the

---

21. This debate originally aired in October 2000. Ankerberg made this statement during the Q & A time. DVD on file.
22. Geisler, *Systematic Theology, vol. 2,* p. 639.
23. Ibid., p. 643.

gap theory and the day-age theory were developed prior to Darwin's *Origin of Species*. Since these views were created in an effort to synthesize the biblical record with scientific opinion, it is obvious that the long periods of time were not an accommodation to evolution.[24] However, it should also be noted that evolutionists today do require long periods of time, and are therefore not open to any young-earth arguments regardless of any scientific data, or (more importantly) the words of Scripture.

Geisler made a more astonishing claim about young-earth creationism when he wrote, "Light was not created on the fourth day, as defenders of the solar day argue; rather it was made on the very first day when God said, 'Let there be light' (Gen. 1:3)."[25] He does not document this claim, so one must wonder where he came up with it. We have never heard of any young-earth creationist making such a biblically ignorant claim.

All young-earthers believe that light was created on the first day, as Genesis says. We differ from old-earthers in that we do not believe this light came from the sun. We believe the sun was not created until the fourth day, precisely as the text states (Gen. 1:16). Young-earthers have consistently made their position clear and have even offered plausible explanations as to what the light on the first three days may have been:

> Where did the light come from? We are not told, but Genesis 1:3 certainly indicates it was a created light to provide day and night until God made the sun on Day 4 to rule the day He had made. Revelation 21:23 tells us that one day the sun will not be needed, because the glory of God will light the heavenly city.[26]

---

24. Neither natural selection nor evolution was discovered or invented by Charles Darwin. He merely proposed the idea that natural selection is the mechanism for producing evolution (i.e., changing one type of organism into another).

25. Geisler, *Systematic Theology*, vol. 2, p. 641. Geisler also makes this statement in his *Baker Encyclopedia of Christian Apologetics* (Grand Rapids, MI: Baker, 1999), p. 271.

26. Ken Ham, ed., *The New Answers Book* (Green Forest, AR: Master Books, 2006), p. 102.

Geisler's statement was made in two books published four years apart, so it cannot be construed as a "typo." Geisler's blunder on this point reveals that he has seriously and inexcusably failed to accurately understand and explain the position he is criticizing.

The Events of Day Six

Old-earth creationists have claimed that there is no way that all of the events of day 6 could have taken place in the span of 24 hours. Gleason Archer summarizes this alleged problem:

> We are told that God created Adam first, gave him the responsibility of tending the Garden of Eden *for some time* until He observed him to be lonely. He then granted him the fellowship of *all the beasts and animals of earth*, with opportunity to bestow names upon them *all*. Some *undetermined period after* that, God observed that Adam *was still lonely* and *finally* fashioned a human wife for him by means of a rib removed from him during a "deep sleep." Then *at last* he brought Eve before Adam and presented her to him as his new life partner. Who can imagine that all of these transactions could possibly have taken place *in 120 minutes* of the sixth day (or even within twenty-four hours, for that matter)? And yet *Gen. 1:27 states that both Adam and Eve were created at the very end of the final day of creation*. Obviously the "days" of chapter 1 are intended to represent stages of unspecified length, not literal twenty-four-hour days.[27]

The italics were added to emphasize the amount of eisegesis performed by Archer on the text. In other words, the italicized words do not appear in the biblical account! Please notice Archer's attempts to add time to this day with the use of words and phrases like "finally," "undetermined period after," and "still lonely." Nowhere does Genesis 2 state that Adam needed to tend the Garden "for some time" before he named the animals. He was assigned the task of tending the Garden (v. 15), but text does not say how big the Garden was or how far Adam got

---

27. Gleason Archer, *A Survey of Old Testament Introduction* (Chicago, IL: Moody Press, 1994, 3rd ed.), p. 201.

in the task before naming the animals and the creation of Eve. Also, the Bible does not say that all of this took place in the final two hours of the sixth day. Neither does Genesis 1:27 claim that Adam and Eve were created at "the very end" of the sixth day. God could have easily created the land animals in the first hour of the day, formed Adam from dust shortly after, and later in the day created Eve from Adam's rib. Archer is reading truckloads into the text, with no contextual justification.

The greatest point of contention in this argument has to do with the naming of the animals. First, the text does not state that Adam had "fellowship" with and named "all the beasts and animals of the earth." This is a common misunderstanding on the part of the old-earthers, due to a failure to observe the text carefully. According to verse 20, Adam only named the cattle, beasts of the field, and birds of the air. He was not responsible for naming the sea creatures, the beasts of the earth, or creeping things (insects, etc.). This would considerably reduce the amount of animals that he had to name. It has been demonstrated that Adam could have easily named each of these creatures in less than four hours, while taking a five-minute break every hour![28]

Despite his eisegetical insertions, other old-earth creationists have followed Archer's example and even added their own ideas. For example, Geisler claims that God's statement, "I will make a helper suitable for him" (Gen. 2:18) implies a period of time between the proclamation and the actual performance.[29] Yet God could have put Adam to sleep immediately after making the statement.

Geisler also attempts to squeeze more time into day six by arguing, "Adam indicated he had anticipated Eve for some time" (Gen. 2:23). Here is what the text actually says, "And Adam said: 'This is now bone of my bones and flesh of my flesh; she shall be called Woman, because she was taken out of Man.'" Where does Adam indicate that he "anticipated Eve for some time"? This argument is based on the idea that the Hebrew word *pah'am* (פַּעַם) can be rendered as "at last." It is true that this is a possible interpretation, but we need to reiterate that the context will determine the meaning. In this particular case, it is

---

28. Andrew Kulikovsky, "How Could Adam Have Named All the Animals in a Single Day?" *Creation* 27:3 (June 2005): p. 27–28.
29. Geisler, *Systematic Theology*, vol. 2, p. 643.

debatable whether it should be rendered this way. In fact, a few Bible translations do include the phrase "at last" in the text but most do not. However, even if the word should be interpreted as "at last," this does not necessarily imply a long period of time. For example, many of us have experienced a hard day at work before. When 5:00 p.m. rolls around we sigh and say, "At last!" In no way does this mean that we worked more than 24 hours (or even more than 8 hours), even if it seemed like "millions of years." In Adam's case, he had just named the animals he was instructed to name and had fallen into a deep sleep. He could have justifiably exclaimed "at last" meaning, "Finally, I have found and can name a creature that can be my mate." These are classic examples of the old-earthers' concerted efforts to deny the plain reading of the text.

Plant "Death"

Old-earthers have tried to avoid the obvious problem of death before sin by claiming that plants must have died prior to Adam's sin. Since Adam, Eve, and the animals used energy, they must have eaten food. Of course, no one would deny that both men and animals ate food before Adam's sin. Genesis 1:29–30 reveals what that food was, when it states that both man and animal were to eat plants. But Hugh Ross argues, "The death of at least plants or plant parts must have occurred before Adam sinned."[30]

In 2004, one of the authors (Jason) participated in a radio debate with Dr. Ross in which Ross pointed to a few Bible verses that speak of plants withering.[31] Of course plants wither. But in what way is that relevant to whether or not they are living things? The Bible does not speak of plants as living things; they are quite different than animals and humans. In fact, the Book of Job poetically contrasts plant "death" with that of a living being — showing that these are two completely different things. In chapter 14 verses 7–10, Job laments that man is not like a tree; when a tree "dies," it can be revived with water, but not so for a man. Plants are not living creatures, and the Bible never refers to them as such.

---

30. Hugh Ross, *A Matter of Days* (Colorado Springs, CO: NavPress, 2004), p. 98.
31. This debate is available at <http://www.answersingenesis.org/Answers Media/play.aspx?mediaID=050125_debate>. Accessed May 1, 2007.

The problem with Ross's argument is not that plants were eaten before the Fall but with his implied claim that plants experienced death in the same sense that animals and humans do. The Bible consistently makes a distinction between animal life and plants. Young-earth creationists point out that only creatures described as *nephesh chayyah* ("living soul" or "living creature") could not have died before the Fall. Plants are never described as *nephesh chayyah*. These Hebrew words are used in Genesis 1:30 to refer to man, every beast of the earth, every bird of the sky, and to every thing that moves on the earth, but in contrast to plants, which are the source of food for all the other creatures. Since plants are not alive in the biblical sense, then they cannot die in the biblical sense, either. Plants should be viewed as a sort of biological machine that God has created to sustain *nephesh* creatures on earth.

Common sense also illustrates the absurdity of Ross's claim. We would rightly be disturbed if a young child were to catch a baby bird and accidentally kill it. However, few would think twice if this same young child picked a flower for his mother — unless it was from her garden! Also, people sit on "dead" trees while on a walk in the woods. But no one would sit on the carcass of a dead animal. We realize there is a drastic difference between animal life and death and plant "life" and "death."

The old-earther cannot escape this serious argument. The Bible is clear that animal and human death came as a result of sin. By placing death before sin (for millions of years), old-earthers are unintentionally impugning God's holy nature. Surely the God who views death as an enemy (1 Cor. 15:26) would not proclaim that a world full of death was "very good" (Gen. 1:31). Yet the old-earthers' views force this contradiction upon the Scriptures.

Revisionist Church History

The debate over the proper interpretation of the creation days is nothing new in Church history. A few church fathers wrote in favor of interpreting the days symbolically; however, the overwhelming consensus among early church fathers was that the days were ordinary days.[32] Dr. Hugh Ross cites the church fathers as support for his view that the days were long periods of time. Among those cited by Ross are "Philo, Josephus, Justin Martyr, Irenaeus, Hippolytus, Ambrose, Origen, Lactantius, Victorinus of Pettau, Methodius of Olympus, Augustine, Eusebius, and Basil the Great."[33] In *The Genesis Question*, Ross claimed:

> Their [Ante-Nicene scholars] comments on the subject [meaning of the word *day* in Genesis 1] remained tentative, with the majority favoring the "long day" (typically a thousand-year period) — apart from the influence of science. Not one explicitly endorsed the twenty-four hour interpretation.[34]

There are several problems with this argument. First, Ross overstates the number of church fathers who allegedly support his view. Philo and Josephus were not church fathers. Ross seems to acknowledge this by listing them in a different subsection. Nevertheless, Philo was a Hellenistic Jew and Josephus was a Jewish general and historian, and he clearly believed in a young earth. Of the others cited, Ambrose, Lactantius, and Methodius favored the literal-day position. Only Philo, Origen, and Augustine clearly questioned or rejected the literal-day view. The remaining fathers were unclear in their writings.[35]

Second, Ross's argument proves too much. Augustine interpreted the days figuratively because he believed that God created everything instantaneously.[36] Rather than supporting an old-earth view, he argued exactly the opposite. Augustine went so far as to write:

> Let us, then, omit the conjectures of men who know not what they say, when they speak of the nature and origin of the

---

32. T. Mortenson, *Orthodoxy and Genesis: What the Fathers Really Taught*. <http://www.answersingenesis.org/tj/v16/i3/orthodoxy.asp>

33. Sarfati, *Refuting Compromise*, p. 108.

34. Hugh Ross, *The Genesis Question*, (Colorado Springs, CO: Navpress, 2001), p. 66.

35. Robert Bradshaw, *Creationism and the Early Church*, <www.robibrad.demon.co.uk/Chapter3.htm>. Accessed May 1, 2007.

36. Ken Ham, ed., *The New Answers Book* (Green Forest, AR: Master Books, 2006), p. 89–90.

human race. . . . They are deceived, too, by those highly men-
dacious documents which profess to give the history of many
thousand years, though, reckoning, by the sacred writings, we
find that not 6,000 years have yet passed.[37]

Augustine attempted to comment on Genesis 1 three different
times during his life. He remained unsure of a proper interpretation of
the word *day* but was quite certain that the earth was young.[38] Augustine also believed in a global flood at the time of Noah in spite of old-
earth views of history at the time.

The Scandal of an Evangelical Mind

Mark Noll's *The Scandal of the Evangelical Mind* raised some
legitimate concerns regarding evangelicalism's inability to influence
modern academia. Unfortunately, Noll spent an entire chapter accus-
ing young-earth creationists of being one of the leading causes behind
this problem. Even though he is considered to be a first-rate historian,
it is alarming to see the amount of misinformation Noll advanced in
this book. Relying heavily on Ronald Numbers' book, *The Creationists*,
Noll claims that young-earth creationism originated with Seventh Day
Adventism.

> [Creationism] has spread like wildfire in our century from
> its humble beginnings in the writings of Ellen White, the
> founder of Seventh-day Adventism, to its current status as a
> gospel truth embraced by tens of millions of Bible-believing
> evangelicals and fundamentalists around the world.[39]

Regrettably, on the very next page Noll again turns to Ronald
Numbers for the following ridiculous claim concerning creationism:

> Numbers described how a fatally flawed interpretive scheme
> [young-earth creationism] of the sort that no responsible

---

37. Augustine, *The City of God*, book 12, chapter 10. Available online at <http://
    www.ccel.org/ccel/schaff/npnf102.iv.XII.10.html>. Accessed May 1, 2007.
38. Mortenson, *The Great Turning Point*, p. 40-41.
39. Mark Noll, *The Scandal of the Evangelical Mind* (Grand Rapids, MI: William
    B. Eerdmans, 1994), p. 13.

Christian teacher in the history of the church ever endorsed before this century came to dominate the minds of American evangelicals on scientific questions.[40]

First, young-earth creationism did not begin with Seventh Day Adventism and the writings of Ellen White (1827–1915). Terry Mortenson analyzed the writings of the "scriptural geologists" of the early 19th century. Many of their biblical and geological arguments against the old-earth geological theories developing at that time are identical to those used by modern young-earthers.[41] George Young was the most accomplished of the "scriptural geologists." A pastor and geologist, he published his first book defending the biblical account of the global flood in 1822 (five years before White was born) and his fullest treatment of the young-earth view, *Scriptural Geology*, in 1838 (when White was only 11). Obviously, Young did not receive his ideas from Ellen White.

In his zeal to blame young-earth creationism for a large portion of evangelical ills, Mark Noll also ignored common sense. By claiming that young-earth creationism was founded on the teachings of Ellen White, he committed the logical error known as the genetic fallacy. The genetic fallacy occurs when one confuses the origin of a view with the truth of the view. It may be a good strategy in a courtroom (i.e., discrediting the witness), but it has no bearing on truth or the validity of an argument. If a discredited witness said that "2+2=4" the statement is still true, even though the witness may be lying or mistaken about other things. Clearly Noll's reasoning here is not logical. Whether or not young-earth creationism began with Ellen White would have no bearing on its truth or falsity. Furthermore, White was taking Genesis 1–11 as literal history just like scriptural geologists did and just as the vast majority of the Church had for the first 18 centuries. Young-earth creationism is nothing new. Rather, old-earth creationism is the novelty and fatally flawed interpretive scheme.

Second, Noll's claim that "no responsible Christian teacher" has ever endorsed young-earth creationism is simply false. Surely Martin

---

40. Ibid., p. 14.
41. Mortenson, *The Great Turning Point*, p. 15.

Luther could be called a "responsible Christian teacher." He made his position on the days of creation clear:

> When Moses writes that God created heaven and earth and whatever is in them in six days, then let this period continue to have been six days, and do not venture to devise any comment according to which six days were one day. But if you cannot understand how this could have been done in six days, then grant the Holy Spirit the honor of being more learned than you are. For you are to deal with Scripture in such a way that you bear in mind that God Himself says what is written. But since God is speaking, it is not fitting for you wantonly to turn His Word in the direction you wish to go.[42]

Luther was not the only "responsible Christian teacher" in Church history who believed the days of Genesis 1 were literal 24-hour days and the earth was approximately 6,000 years old. John Calvin wrote:

> For it is not without significance that he divided the making of the universe into six days, even though it would have been no more difficult for him to have completed in one moment the whole work together in all its details than to arrive at its completion gradually by a progression of this sort.[43]

In this statement, Calvin explicitly denied an instantaneous creation, which was a view in his day. Calvin's use of the word *day* was obviously referring to a normal day of 24 hours. For example, he wrote, "They will not refrain from guffaws when they are informed that but little more than five thousand years have passed since the creation of the universe."[44]

As mentioned earlier, the early Church fathers Ambrose, Lactantius, and Methodius believed in a young earth. In fact, the majority of Church leaders throughout history have favored this view. This is

---

42. *What Luther Says. A Practical In-Home Anthology for the Active Christian*, compiled by Ewald M. Plass (St. Louis, MO: Concordia, 1959), p. 1523.
43. John Calvin, *Institutes of the Christian Religion*, J.T. McNeill, editor (Philadelphia, PA: Westminster Press, 1960), 1.14.22
44. Calvin, *Institutes*, 2:925.

why there is such a lack of discussion on the early chapters of Genesis in all of the early commentaries. There was no debate about it because the commentators took Genesis at face value and accepted the young-earth view. Mark Noll is seriously wrong on this entire point. Sadly, his book has influenced the Church significantly to reject the plain truth of Genesis. So just where is the scandalous misuse of the Christian mind?

Improper View of General and Special Revelation

God has chosen to reveal himself to man through various means, which can be divided into two categories: general and special revelation. General revelation consists of information that has been available to all people throughout all time. God's creation and man's conscience are sources of general revelation, according to Romans 1:18–20 and 2:14–15; Acts 14:15–17 and 17:24–29; Job 12:7–10; Psalm 19:1 and 97:6. Dr. Ross incorrectly claims that modern scientific discoveries are a source of general revelation. However, since this information was not readily available to all people in history, it cannot be. Special revelation consists of the Word of God. This includes the Bible and Jesus Christ when He walked the earth. General revelation confronts us with the existence and at least some of the characteristics of God. But nowhere does the Bible say that we can work out the history of the creation simply by studying the creation. According to Romans 1:20, general revelation can provide enough information to condemn a person. Only special revelation reveals to us that salvation comes by faith in Jesus Christ and His finished work. Obviously, both are helpful tools in evangelism but Christians must be careful to keep them in proper perspective.

Some old-earthers are guilty of elevating general revelation to the same level as special revelation. Ross contends:

> God's revelation is not limited exclusively to the Bible's words. The facts of nature may be likened to a sixty-seventh book of the Bible. . . . Some readers might feel that I am implying that God's revelation through nature is somehow on an equal footing with His revelation through the words of the Bible. Let me simply state that truth, by definition, is information that is perfectly free of contradiction and error. Just as it

is absurd to speak of some entity as more perfect than another,
so also one revelation of God's truth cannot be held as inferior
or superior to another.[45]

Even though Ross attempts to deny that he is placing general revelation on par with special revelation, he is doing exactly that. Ross also
errs in what he calls general revelation, as he confuses his interpretation
of nature with fact.

An important distinction must be made. God's creation is suffering from 6,000 years of the Curse, while Scripture is "God-breathed"
and therefore inerrant and not cursed (2 Tim. 3:16). General revelation
cannot be "likened to a sixty-seventh book of the Bible" because nature
is cursed. This does not mean that it cannot provide man with accurate
information, but it does mean that it is not of the same caliber as God's
Word. One of Ross's favorite Bible passages unmistakably illustrates
this point. Psalm 19:1 pronounces, "The heavens declare the glory of
God and the firmament shows His handiwork." The Psalmist is speaking of general revelation here and says that it testifies to the existence
and majesty of the Creator. Nevertheless, a few verses later, the Psalmist reveals that God's Word is superior. "The law of the Lord is perfect,
converting the soul" (Ps. 19:7). Notice it is special revelation that is
capable of "converting the soul." Verses 9 and 10 of the same Psalm add
that God's judgments (part of special revelation) are to be desired more
than gold and honey (part of general revelation).

The old-earth creationist has made another theological error in
putting general and special revelation at the same level. In Matthew
24:35, Jesus stated, "Heaven and earth will pass away, but My words
will by no means pass away." In this statement, "heaven and earth"
are a part of general revelation. These things are going to "pass away"
but Jesus specifically taught that His words, which are a part of special
revelation, will never pass away. As such, it is impossible to liken nature
"to a sixty-seventh book of the Bible."

To this rebuttal, the old-earther may claim, as Walter Kaiser did,
that the interpreter of God's Word is also suffering from the Curse.[46]

---

45. Ross, *Creation and Time*, p. 56–57.
46. The Great Debate, Program 6.

This is true. But again, the argument proves too much. If he is trying to say that because of this no one can be sure of any interpretation, then he has just undermined his entire career as a seminary professor. If all he is trying to say is that the interpreter is fallible, then his argument still falls short. It would be far better for a fallible interpreter to attempt to interpret the infallible record, the Bible, than it would be for the same fallible interpreter to attempt to interpret a fallible record, such as a cursed world. Added to that, the vast majority of young-earthers are God-fearing people who want to interpret Scripture in a way that is pleasing to God. Old-earthers are relying on the interpretations of nature by people who for the most part are God-haters who could not care less about what God thinks of their interpretations. Only through the corrective lens of God's infallible Word can one make proper sense of the cursed world.

Conclusion to the First Round of Proceedings

Young-earth creationism clearly has the upper hand when only the Bible is consulted. This idea is bolstered by the comments of old-earthers such as Pattle Pun and Gleason Archer (quoted earlier), who admit that young-earth creationism seems to be the plain meaning of the biblical text — without considering "science." As such, for old-earth views to be accepted as the proper interpretation of God's Word, two things must be done.

First, since Scripture cannot contradict Scripture, old-earthers must show that the young-earth creationist view is at odds with other portions of Scripture. This has never been done. Young-earthers can point to several passages that become problematic when one adopts an old-earth interpretation of Genesis 1.[47] As a result, young-earth creationism stands on solid theological ground, whereas old-earth creationism has been built on a sandy foundation.

Second, old-earthers must also show that their hermeneutic is just as sound, if not better, than the young-earth creationists' hermeneutic. It has been demonstrated in this first section that old-earthers force interpretations on numerous passages, which cannot be defended from the context. In other words, just because a word, such as *yom*, can be

---

47. See Appendix B for more on this subject.

interpreted to mean a long period of time in a few contexts does not mean that it should be interpreted that way in other contexts. Again, the context of the passage determines the meaning. This issue of context will come into play in even greater detail in the next section.

From what we have seen thus far, we can conclude that young-earth creationism has very strong scriptural support. It is based on sound exegesis of the text. On the other hand, old-earth creationism is based on eisegesis. In other words, the old-earther has to add his ideas to Scripture in order to come away with the desired interpretation. Young-earth creationism has easily won the first round of proceedings.

Chapter 5

Prosecution —
Extent of the Flood

Often overlooked in the debate between old-earth creationists and young-earth creationists is the biblical account of the Flood. John Ankerberg hosted a debate between young-earthers Ken Ham and Dr. Jason Lisle and old-earthers Dr. Walter Kaiser and Dr. Hugh Ross on the *John Ankerberg Show*. This debate was filmed in January 2006 and began airing later the same month. Of the ten sessions available on DVD, only a portion of one session was devoted to this topic. This is unfortunate, because the topic of the Flood is inexorably linked with the battle over the days of Genesis.

Young-earth creationists contend that Genesis clearly teaches that the Flood was a worldwide, cataclysmic event. In other words, every single piece of earth throughout the entire world was under water at the same time. The only land-dwelling creatures that survived this Flood were those on board the ark. It is important to understand the extent of the Flood, because many old-earthers use ambiguous language. For example, Dr. Hugh Ross claims to believe in what he calls a "universal" Flood. By this, however, he means that God sent a geographically localized flood that destroyed everything that had come into contact with sinful humans, who at the time (Ross believes) were only living in the Mesopotamian valley (roughly modern-day Iraq). He reasons that there would be no need for God to wipe out Antarctica and its animal inhabitants, because man had not ventured that far yet. These ideas will be examined in chapter 6.

This topic is crucial for another reason. The old-earth creation model accepts secular dating estimates of fossils and rock layers. Hence, old-earth creationists believe that most of the fossils and sedimentary rock layers on earth were laid down over millions of years. However, young-earth geologists have pointed out that a worldwide flood could also account for these features — without the need for millions of years. Certainly, a global flood would kill billions of organisms and trap them in layers of sediment, accounting for the sedimentary rock layers and fossils we see today. So, a global flood means the fossils and rocks are not millions of years old; they are powerful evidence for a young earth. Conversely, if the rocks and fossils really were millions of years old, then there cannot have been a worldwide flood — since such a violent Flood would destroy any previous fossil record. Old-earth creationists therefore must deny a global flood in order for their position to make any sense.

A great deal of research has been done by young-earth creationists confirming that a worldwide flood can account for earth's amazingly diverse topography. It is beyond the scope of this book to examine all the scientific evidence in this field; nonetheless, several examples are provided in chapter 7. Here, the biblical evidence for a worldwide deluge will be presented.

The worldwide extent of the Genesis flood can easily be established from looking at the text. Numerous verses testify to the total destruction that would come upon the whole earth. Genesis 6–9 provides the historical account of the event so we will start there.

"All Flesh"

In Genesis 6:5, we are informed that man's wickedness was exceedingly great. As a result, God decided to judge the world to put an end to this wickedness. He said in verse 7, "I will destroy man whom I have created from the face of the earth, both man and beast, creeping thing and birds of the air, for I am sorry that I have made them." It is clear that God's judgment extended from mankind to the birds and land animals.

The fact that all non-marine creatures were wiped out is repeated several times. God said in Genesis 6:13 that it would be "the end of all flesh" except for those on the ark. A few verses later He qualified this statement by saying that the Flood would "destroy from under heaven all flesh in which is the breath of life; everything that is on the earth shall die" (v. 17). God said that He would "destroy from the face of the earth all living things that [he had] made" (Gen. 7:4). Genesis 7:21–23 declares:

> And all flesh died that moved on the earth: birds and cattle and beasts and every creeping thing that creeps on the earth, and every man. All in whose nostrils was the breath of the spirit of life, all that was on the dry land, died. So He destroyed all living things which were on the face of the ground: both man and cattle, creeping thing and bird of the air. They were destroyed from the earth. Only Noah and those who were with him in the ark remained alive.

These verses alone should be enough to discredit any notion that the Bible endorses a local flood.

The Size of the Ark

In Genesis 6:15, God instructed Noah to build a huge boat. He said, "The length of the ark shall be three hundred cubits, its width fifty cubits, and its height thirty cubits." A cubit is a unit of measure roughly equal to the distance from a person's elbow to the tip of his middle finger. Scholars believe the standard cubit was 17.5–18 inches. If the 18-inch cubit is correct, then the ark would have been 450 feet long by 75 feet high by 45 feet tall. With these dimensions, the ark would have had a volume of 1.52 million cubit feet.

Why would God tell Noah to build such an enormous boat if He were only going to flood the Mesopotamian region? Noah could have housed all of the local fauna on a much smaller vessel. What is even more perplexing is that God told Noah to build a boat at all if it were just a local flood. Why did God not tell Noah to move instead? We don't know exactly how long it took Noah to build the ark, but it seems likely that it took many years. This would have been more than enough time to move his family and the animals to a region that was not going to be flooded. In fact, he would have only needed a few weeks or months to walk out of the region.

Dr. Hovind asked Dr. Ross these questions during their debate on the *John Ankerberg Show*. Ross responded with a highly improbable *ad hoc* argument which is not found anywhere in the text. He said that it was because "God always provides His preachers a pulpit to preach from."[1] Where does the Bible say that this was the purpose for the ark?

This point needs special attention. Noah was told to bring two of every kind of bird on board the ark. Most birds are more than capable of escaping local floods because they have the ability to quickly fly out of the region experiencing the flood. Most land animals could have easily exited the region as well. The idea of a local flood is completely inconsistent with the commands God gave to Noah and makes a subtle attack at God's nature. Why would God cause Noah to spend years of his life building an enormous and completely unnecessary ark? Moreover, the Bible specifically states that the purpose of putting animals on the ark was to keep them alive (Gen. 7:2–3, 6:19–20).

The Flood Waters

The Bible provides specific details about the Flood itself. At the start of the Flood, we are told that "the fountains of the great deep were broken up, and the windows of heaven were opened" (Gen. 7:11). The next verse states that it rained for 40 days and 40 nights. In these two verses we are given the sources of the water. The "fountains of the great deep" may be a reference to volcanic and geyser activity. The opening of the "windows of heaven" indicates water from the sky — torrential rainfall.

Genesis 7:18–20 provides some interesting details of the Flood waters.

> The waters prevailed and greatly increased on the earth, and the ark moved about on the surface of the waters. And the waters prevailed exceedingly on the earth, and all the high hills

---

1. Dr. Hugh Ross, "The Age of the Earth" on the *John Ankerberg Show*, October 2000.

under the whole heaven were covered. The waters prevailed fifteen cubits upward, and the mountains were covered.

Notice that even the mountains were covered. Once this occurred, the Flood could not have been a local event. Water will level itself out. Even if the Flood started in just Mesopotamia, it would have gone worldwide as soon as the mountains were covered.

Genesis 8:4 reports that the ark came to rest on "the mountains of Ararat." The text does not say that it was specifically on Mt. Ararat. Instead it landed on a mountain in the region of Ararat (eastern Turkey today). However, the point is still the same. The ark landed on a mountaintop. Obviously, the water level was much higher than would ever be obtained by a local flood. Also, it was another two and a half months before the tops of the surrounding mountains were seen (Gen. 8:5). Certainly, the mountain upon which the ark landed was the highest in the region at the time. So, even though the text does not explicitly say it was Mt. Ararat, many scholars believe it is the most likely candidate for the final resting place of Noah's ark.

Another strong reason for believing that the Flood was global is the duration of the Flood. Many believers have mistakenly assumed

that it only lasted 40 days and 40 nights. This is based on a misreading of Genesis 7:12. It is true that the heavy rains lasted this long, but the Flood itself was much longer. Genesis 8:2 seems to indicate that it continued to rain throughout the first 150 days. Perhaps the first 40 days represented the initial downpour and then it continued to rain on a regular basis just as it does today. Bear in mind that the Flood also received water from "the fountains of the great deep."

The Bible states that the Flood began "in the six hundredth year of Noah's life, in the second month, the seventeenth day of the month" (Gen. 7:11). The Flood waters "prevailed on the earth" for the next 150 days (Gen. 7:24). The waters began to subside and the ark came to rest ten days later (Gen. 8:4). The surface of the ground finally dried up on the first day of the first month of Noah's six hundred and first year (Gen. 8:13). This was 313 days after the rain began! Noah waited until the 27th day of the second month before disembarking (Gen. 8:14). In total, Noah and his family were on the ark for over a year — 371 days to be exact!

The sheer length of the Flood testifies to its global character. No local flood has ever lasted anywhere close to this long. Most local floods only last a few days to a few weeks. It seems preposterous to conclude that the Bible was speaking of something other than a worldwide catastrophe. This brings us to yet another powerful piece of evidence for a global flood.

The Rainbow

Following the Flood, God entered into a covenant with His faithful servant, Noah. As a symbol of that covenant, God provided the rainbow. Pay close attention to the following account from Genesis 9:12–17.

> And God said: "This is the sign of the covenant which I make between Me and you, and every living creature that is with you, for perpetual generations: I set My rainbow in the cloud, and it shall be for the sign of the covenant between Me and the earth. It shall be, when I bring a cloud over the earth, that the rainbow shall be seen in the cloud; and I will remember My covenant which is between Me and you and

every living creature of all flesh; the waters shall never again become a flood to destroy all flesh. The rainbow shall be in the cloud, and I will look on it to remember the everlasting covenant between God and every living creature of all flesh that is on the earth." And God said to Noah, "This is the sign of the covenant which I have established between Me and all flesh that is on the earth."

The rainbow was given as a promise from God that He would never send a flood to "destroy all flesh." If this were just referring to a local flood, then God has lied every single time someone sees a rainbow in the sky. In this case, He has repeatedly broken His promise, because local floods that kill some animals and people are very common on earth.

Earlier it was mentioned that old-earth theology impugns God's nature by insisting on millions of years because it necessarily places death before sin. Here again, the old-earthers who argue for a local flood are (inadvertently) attacking the character of our holy Creator by implying that He has lied repeatedly. Many old-earthers may simply be unaware of their serious error in this area and need to carefully examine the grave consequences of accepting such an anti-biblical concept.

Big Changes

So far we have examined some of the obvious arguments for a worldwide flood. Now it is time to look at some subtle evidences for it. The Flood had a tremendous impact on the earth. When Noah stepped off the ark, it would have been a very different environment; the world he knew was gone (see 2 Pet. 3:6). Therefore, God instituted major changes after the Flood. Life on earth was going to be drastically different than it was before the Flood.

In Genesis 9:3, God instituted a change in the diets of people. He said, "Every moving thing that lives shall be food for you. I have given you all things, even as the green herbs." The "green herbs" is a reference to the original command given to Adam in Genesis 1:29. This verse reveals that mankind was originally only allowed to eat plants. Genesis 1:30 prescribes a vegetarian diet for all of the animals. Since the time of the Flood, man has been allowed to eat meat, but carnivorous activity among the animals may have started soon after Adam and Eve sinned. As far as humanity is concerned, the Flood wrought enormous changes.

The post-Flood landscape would have been vastly different than the pre-Flood world. Many Christians make the mistake of assuming the Garden of Eden existed in the Middle East between the Tigris and Euphrates Rivers. After all, they reason, Genesis 2:14 mentions both of these rivers. The problem with this view is that Genesis 2 says that one river went out of the Garden and then was divided into four rivers, two of which were called the Tigris and Euphrates. The other two rivers were called the Pishon and the Gihon (Gen. 2:10–13). Nothing in the Middle East matches this geographical description. This is problematic for those who believe in a local flood but is what one should expect if the whole world was destroyed by water. Earth's entire topography would have been completely reworked.

The question naturally arises as to why the Tigris and Euphrates are named. There is an easy explanation for this. After leaving the mountains of Ararat, the post-Flood settlers would have named places and landmarks based on what they already knew. This is the same reason that the United States has places named Birmingham (Alabama), Moscow (Idaho), and Plymouth (Massachusetts), etc. These cities were named after places familiar to emigrants from England, Russia, and elsewhere. It makes perfect sense that those settling the world after the Flood would have done the same thing.

The changed landscape also puts to rest one of the critics' most common arguments. Dr. Ross often uses this straw-man argument in an attempt to make the global flood look silly. He wrote, "To cover Mount Everest (elevation 29,028 feet, or 8,848 meters) with water would require four and a half times the total water resources of the entire planet."[2] This argument demonstrates Ross's acceptance of uniformitarian principles.[3] He is looking at the present world and assuming that the pre-Flood world was the same, or at least very similar. Young-earth creationists do not believe that Mount Everest existed

---

2. Ross, *The Genesis Question*, p. 148.
3. The acceptance of uniformitarian principles is responsible for many of the scientific mistakes made by old-earth creationists. Chapter 8 deals with these kinds of arguments.

prior to the Flood. The Bible indicates that at the end of the Flood "the mountains rose, the valleys sank down" (Ps. 104:8, NASB).

This illustrates a very important principle. When one starts from the Bible, then all of these so-called difficulties can be answered. This makes perfect sense. God is infinite in wisdom and knowledge. He was there throughout history and He told us what happened. Of course His Word should be accurate.

Arguments from Other Books of the Bible

So far we have presented evidence only from the Book of Genesis. Many more arguments could have been given from Genesis but will be covered in the next chapter when responding to local flood arguments. It is now time to examine the evidence provided by the rest of Scripture.

Special Words

The Old Testament uses a particular word to describe the Flood. The word "flood" occurs 39 times in the New King James Version of the Old Testament. Our English word "flood" translates several different Hebrew words. However, whenever the flood of Noah's day is described, it uses the word *mabbuwl* (מבול). This word occurs 13 times in the Old Testament, and every time it appears it refers specifically to the Genesis flood.[4] The Hebrew language has other words, such as *nachal* (נחל) or *mayim* (מים), to describe the kinds of local floods we see today. It is as if the Hebrew writers were making it very clear that the flood of Noah's day was entirely unique.

The same thing occurs in the New Testament. The Greek language has several words that could properly be interpreted as "flood." For example, the following words are all rendered as "flood" by the New King James Version: *potamos, plemmura, anachusis,* and *kataklusmos*. Of these four words, only *kataklusmos* (from which we get our word cataclysm) is used to refer to the Genesis flood. Once again, it is as if the Bible writers were setting this Flood apart from any other flood in earth's history.

The apostle Peter mentioned the Flood in both of his brief letters. In his first epistle, he mentioned that only "eight souls" were saved

---

4. See Genesis 6:17; 7:6, 7, 10, 17; 9:11, 15, 28; 10:1, 32; 11:10; and Psalm 29:10.

during the Flood (1 Pet. 3:20). In his second letter, Peter elaborates on the Flood. He wrote that the original creation was flooded with water and "perished" (2 Pet. 3:6). Remember, this is one of the three events Peter prophesied that uniformitarian scoffers would "deliberately forget" (2 Pet. 3:5, NIV).

Jumping Ship

Local flood theorists have another severe difficulty to overcome. Many of their old-earth allies have abandoned them when it comes to this topic. For example, some of the leading scholars mentioned in earlier chapters seem to favor a worldwide flood. Dr. Norman Geisler and Dr. Gleason Archer are just two of the many evangelical scholars who have accepted an old earth but apparently do not accept the local flood idea.

Ironically, old-earthers who do believe in a worldwide flood fail to see the inconsistency in their thinking. The idea of billions of years came from the uniformitarian interpretation of the rock layers. Allegedly, it takes a long time for these layers to build up to the point they are today. The inconsistency lies in the fact that a worldwide flood would easily be capable of depositing the sedimentary layers of rock that are observed. The Flood would have also preserved the fossilized remains of countless organisms. So, if there was a worldwide flood, then there is no need for the billions of years. On the other hand, if the fossil record is indeed a record of billions of years of earth history, then a worldwide flood is impossible. The Genesis flood would have reworked the sediments and thus destroyed any alleged record of earth's ancient past.

In a futile attempt to overcome this difficulty, some old-earthers have proposed a global but tranquil flood. But a global tranquil flood is an oxymoron. Look at the catastrophic effects of local flooding such as the Asian tsunami on December 26, 2004, or the tragic destruction of New Orleans by Hurricane Katrina in August 2005. The eruption of Mount St. Helens in May 1980 also produced tremendous geologic changes in the region as a result of the subsequent flooding, and yet this volcanic eruption was a relatively small one. These were major disasters with extremely tragic results, but they were only local or regional disasters. Try to imagine what a worldwide flood accompanied by "all the fountains of the great deep" bursting forth would do to this world. There simply is no such thing as a tranquil flood, let alone a tranquil worldwide flood.

The Ark as a Type of Christ

One of the interesting aspects of the ark is its comparison to Christ in the New Testament. The ark was literally the only means of physical salvation for all of its occupants. All who failed to board the ark were swept away to destruction. In the same way, Jesus Christ is the only way of salvation (John 14:6). All who fail to trust in Him alone for salvation will be sentenced to everlasting destruction. In a very subtle way, the local flood idea strikes against the concept of Jesus being the only way to the Father. If the Flood had been merely a local event, then every creature outside of the flooded region did not need to board the ark. If this were the case, then one might justifiably wonder if another means of salvation is provided besides the Lord Jesus Christ.

Thankfully, the local flood theorists are not this consistent, at least those who would be considered theological conservatives. They are typically just as adamant as young-earthers that Jesus Christ is the only way to the Father.

The prosecution has made its initial case for the universality and worldwide nature of the Genesis flood. It is time to see if the local flood theorists can successfully answer these arguments and make a legitimate case for their claims.

Chapter 6

Defense —
A Local Flood?

As mentioned in the previous chapter, if they are to be consistent, old-earth creationists are forced to believe in a local flood. Can they provide adequate responses to the prosecution's case presented in the last chapter? We shall see. Perhaps the two leading promoters of the local flood idea are Dr. Hugh Ross and Davis A. Young. Ross is the founder of a ministry called *Reasons to Believe* and Young is a professor of geology at Calvin College.

What Is a "Universal" Flood?

Dr. Ross often claims that the Flood was universal but not global. You may be wondering exactly what that means, so we will allow Ross to explain himself.

> Any flood that exterminates all human beings, all the soulish animals with whom they have contact, and all their material possessions — except those on board Noah's Ark — would be universal and would achieve God's purpose in pouring out judgment.[1]

---

1. Dr. Hugh Ross, *The Genesis Question* (Colorado Springs, CO: NavPress, 1998), p. 140.

By using the term "soulish," Ross is referring to those creatures that are described in the Hebrew language as *nephesh chayyah*. His view is that the Flood destroyed all of humanity, except Noah and his family, and every *nephesh* creature that had come into contact with fallen humanity. He explains:

> If no people lived in Antarctica [prior to the Flood], God would have no reason to destroy the place or its penguins. Nor would Noah be required to take a pair of Emperor penguins aboard the ark.[2]

This view has some serious problems. First, Ross assumes that Antarctica existed before the Flood. This demonstrates his acceptance of the uniformitarian philosophy — the present is the key to the past. It was demonstrated in the previous chapter that the pre-Flood world was much different than the post-Flood world.

Second, Ross did not obtain this idea from the text. Ross begins his argument this way:

> Determining the extent of the great Flood that eradicated all humanity except Noah and his family will depend on discovering the extent to which the population (thus, the wickedness) had spread by Noah's time. My first approach to this determination is simple: Through science we can deduce that pre-Flood humans never settled Antarctica.[3]

This is typical for Ross, even though he often claims that his ideas come from Scripture. We have studied a number of his debates, and he almost always argues this way. Scientific arguments are given first, as though they are the authority to which all others must bow, and then he cites the text in an effort to justify his scientific opinions. In this particular case, his conclusion is based on his belief that there was never a worldwide flood on earth. Remember, the Bible clearly teaches a worldwide catastrophe. The local flood theorists' views on the biblical text will be dealt with shortly.

---

2. Ross, *The Genesis Question*, p. 140.
3. Ibid., p. 141.

Finally, Ross implies that somehow sin's impact was limited to man, his belongings, his locale, and his animals. Yet the Bible teaches that all of creation "groans and labors with birth pangs" because of man's sin (Rom. 8:22). We have noticed that old-earth theology has a tendency to minimize the effects of sin. After all, if death, suffering, disease, bloodshed, thorns, and thistles were already in the world before Adam sinned, then what did sin do? It seems that sin had very little impact on the world in old-earth theology. Yet, a straightforward reading of the Bible indicates that sin ruined the original paradise.

A Limited Curse?

Some old-earth creationists have claimed that the curse on the ground (Gen. 3:17–19) was limited to the Garden of Eden. Based on comments made during the 2006 Ankerberg debate, it seems Ross shares this view as well. He claimed that Adam knew what death and thorns were based on his experience in the world before God placed him in the Garden of Eden.[4] Ross believes that it would have been impossible for Adam to have known what death and thorns were if he did not have prior experience with them.

Once again, this argument just fails to hold up when exposed to the light of Scripture. The third chapter of Genesis provides the account of the Fall. Adam and Eve ate the forbidden fruit and consequently God punished them and the serpent. Verses 17b–19 state:

> Cursed is the ground for your sake; in toil you shall eat of it all the days of your life. Both thorns and thistles it shall bring forth for you, and you shall eat the herb of the field. In the sweat of your face you shall eat bread till you return to the ground, for out of it you were taken; for dust you are, and to dust you shall return.

Notice there is no indication of a limited curse. God said it was "the ground" that was cursed for Adam's sake. Ross interprets this to mean that God was only talking about the Garden of Eden. This simply is not true. God said that Adam would return to "the ground" from which he was taken. In context this is the same ground that God said

---

4. *The Great Debate*, Program 3.

He would curse; the Hebrew term *adamah* is used both times. God did not curse only the ground of the Garden of Eden with thorns, for that is the area from which Adam was expelled. God cursed the ground that Adam was expelled to and the ground to which he would return after death. That was all the ground outside the Garden.

There is another problem with this argument. When Noah was born, his father Lamech said, "This one will comfort us concerning our work and the toil of our hands, because of the ground which the Lord has cursed" (Gen. 5:29). Once again, we see that the ground was cursed (and the same Hebrew words for "ground" and "cursed" are used). This ground could not have been the Garden of Eden, since God had placed cherubim at the edge of the Garden to keep man from reentering it (Gen. 3:24). We can be sure that Lamech did not overpower these cherubim so that he could live in the Garden again. The Bible is clear on this point: all of the ground was cursed because of man's sin. There was no limit to the extent of the curse, as Ross claims.

A Different Approach

Davis Young does not agree with Dr. Ross concerning the extent of the Flood. Interestingly enough, he does not even agree with his own earlier writings. In 1977, he wrote *Creation and the Flood,* in which he promoted the idea of a global yet tranquil flood.[5] He now believes in a local flood but he differs with Ross because he does not believe that it wiped out all of mankind. Young has abandoned one bad idea for another one. This is a common practice among those who insist on allowing man's fallible teachings to be their guide rather than the unchanging Word of God. Here is Young's view in his own words:

> But archeological investigations have established the presence of human beings in the Americas, Australia, and southeastern Asia long before the advent of the sort of Near Eastern civilization described in the Bible and thus long before the biblical deluge could have taken place. In the light of a wealth of mutually supportive evidence from a variety of disciplines and sources, it is simply no longer tenable to insist that a

5. Davis A. Young, *Creation and the Flood* (Grand Rapids, MI: Baker, 1977), p. 172–174, 210–212.

deluge drowned every human on the face of the globe except Noah's family.[6]

Young does not accept that the Flood wiped out all of humanity because he believes that people have been living in the "Americas, Australia, and southeastern Asia" since well before the timing of the Genesis flood. He believes this "fact" has been well established by several disciplines of science, which he calls "extra-biblical" evidence.

First, notice that Young's rejection of a worldwide flood is based on secular scientific majority opinion rather than the text itself. In fact, Young seems to imply that the New Testament authors believed in a worldwide flood! He wrote, "These New Testament writers clearly assumed the historical existence of Noah and the deluge, and they viewed the deluge as a unique event." The only way this event could have been unique is if it were worldwide, since there have been countless local floods, some of them quite large in geographic extent.

Think about that for a minute. If the New Testament authors accepted a global flood, and wrote about it, then why would Young reject it? Is he actually claiming that the Bible is wrong? Yes, indirectly! First Peter 3:20 clearly states that only eight people survived the Flood. Young does not accept this even though there is strong "extra-biblical" support for a worldwide flood.

Literally hundreds of ancient cultures tell of a massive worldwide flood in which only one family survived, with animals, on a large boat. It is true that many of these accounts sound legendary and mythical, but these things often have a basis in truth. This becomes very intriguing when one examines the points of similarity in these stories. In fact, many of these ancient stories are not limited to the Flood. Some of these cultures tell stories that correspond to the major events of the first 11 chapters of the Bible, such as the creation, the fall of Adam and Eve, the Flood, and the Tower of Babel.

In 1997, Ethel Nelson, a missionary to China, published *God's Promise to the Chinese* in which she demonstrated how the ancient Chinese language, through its use of picture-characters instead of letters,

6. Davis A. Young, *The Biblical Flood: A Case Study of the Church's Response to Extrabiblical Evidence* (Grand Rapids, MI: William B. Eerdmans Publishing, 1995), p. 242.

revealed their knowledge of creation and the Flood.[7] This fascinating discovery lends tremendous "extra-biblical" support for the veracity of Genesis.

Sadly, while claiming to uphold biblical inerrancy, Young soundly rejects it in his writings. He calls for a reinterpretation of Genesis 6–9 even though he recognizes that his view is contrary to the Church's historic position on this issue. Young's changing views of the Flood provide a strong example of how dangerous it is to compromise God's Word with changing (secular) scientific opinion.

Redefining Words and Phrases

We come now to the first real purportedly biblical argument offered by local flood theorists. Dr. Ross claims that when the reader sees phrases such as "under the entire heavens" and "every living thing on the face of the earth," we must learn to "interpret in light of their [the authors'] frame of reference, not ours."[8] In other words, when the Bible claims that "all the high hills under the whole of heaven were covered" (Gen. 7:19), we must interpret it through the eyes of Noah. From his vantage point, it looked like all the mountaintops were covered, so it would be safe for the biblical author to write it this way without being accused of error.

In support of this view, Ross cites a few passages which most scholars do interpret this way. Genesis 41:56 speaks of the seven-year famine during Joseph's life. It states, "The famine was over all the face of the earth." It is true that most commentators would view this as hyperbole. The author did not really mean that every single part of the earth was enduring the famine. Instead, the world known to the Egyptians, or perhaps the author, was suffering from the famine. He

> **Hyperbole** — a figure of speech in which the author exaggerates for emphasis.

also cites Romans 1:8 in which Paul wrote, ". . . your faith is spoken of throughout the whole world." Again, the reader is not to think that the Native Americans heard about the faith of the Roman Christians.

---

7. Ethel R. Nelson, *God's Promise to the Chinese* (Dunlap, TN: Read Books Publishers, 1997).

8. Ross, *The Genesis Question*, p. 142.

We do not know of any commentator, old-earth or young-earth, who would dispute that hyperbole is used many times in the Bible.

Nevertheless, the burden of proof still falls on Ross because "all" and "every" do often have an absolute sense. For example, when Romans 3:23 says all have sinned, that is not hyperbole — literally all (each and every one) people have sinned. Jesus literally has all authority in heaven and on earth (Matt. 28:18) and literally every knee will bow to acknowledge Him as Lord one day (Phil. 2:11). Furthermore, a cursory reading of Genesis 6–9 reveals numerous references to total destruction. For Ross's view to be correct, every single one of these must be interpreted as hyberbole. Some verses contain two words or phrases that indicate a worldwide event. Ross cited Genesis 7:19 as an example of hyperbole. It reads, "And the waters prevailed exceedingly on the earth, and all the high hills under the whole heaven were covered." Of course, Ross wants the phrase "all the high hills" to refer to a local area. This interpretation simply cannot be because the text says all of the high hills under "the whole heaven" were covered. The second phrase demonstrates conclusively that the text is not simply referring to all the hills of the area, but rather all the hills under the entire sky (the "whole heaven") (i.e., all the high hills on earth). In order for Dr. Ross's view to be correct, *both* of these phrases would have to be hyperbole, when the context shows that neither one of them is. Verse 20 adds, "The waters prevailed fifteen cubits upward, and the mountains were covered." Not only did the water cover the mountains, it was some 22 feet (15 cubits) above the top of the highest mountain in existence at the time.

Ross would have us believe that the confusion is due to the "small vocabulary" of the Hebrew language. He states, "The translators' wording of this passage [Gen. 7:19–20] explains why so many English-speaking Christians firmly conclude that the Flood must have been global." [9] He then goes on to quote the King James Version and the New International Version to show why so many "English-speaking Christians" reach the global flood conclusion. For Ross, the debate hinges on the proper translation of the word translated as "covered" (Hebrew *kacah* כָּסָה). He claims that all of the English translators

9. Ross, *The Genesis Question*, p. 145.

were "influenced, unawares, by preconceptions about the story."[10] In other words, the English translators believed in a global flood so they mistakenly, yet unintentionally, translated this passage to support their view. He cites the *Theological Wordbook of the Old Testament* in which R. Laird Harris states, "In Gen. 7:19–20 the hills were 'covered'; the Hebrew does not specify with what. The NIV specification of water goes beyond the Hebrew."[11]

With all due respect, perhaps it is Harris and Ross who have been influenced by their own preconceptions about the story and are not reading the biblical text very carefully. If it were not so misleading, it would be laughable that Harris claims that the hills were covered but "the Hebrew does not specify with what." What else could have covered the mountains to a depth of 15 cubits? This passage is right in the middle of a graphic description of the Flood! The translators had very good reasons for translating this passage in the way they did. The Hebrew word for water (*mayim*) appears in both verses! Obviously, the water covered the mountains to this depth.

In addition, there are references to complete destruction, which cannot be interpreted hyperbolically. For example, in Genesis 6:7 God declared, "I will destroy man whom I have created from the face of the earth, both man and beast, creeping thing and birds of the air, for I am sorry that I have made them." Ross accepts that God was going to wipe out all of humanity with the exception of Noah and his family. This verse puts the land animals and birds in the same context as mankind. They were all going to be destroyed. How does he justify his belief that God would not destroy Antarctica or its penguins? Not from the text. His views are based on his acceptance of secular scientific opinions. As sad as it may seem, all of the penguins, except for those on the ark, were killed during the Flood, despite Ross's reasoning. And besides this, penguins don't just live in Antarctica. They are found on every continent in the Southern Hemisphere, including the southwest coast of Africa and the west

---

10. Ibid.
11. Robert Laird Harris, Gleason Leonard Archer, and Bruce K. Waltke, *Theological Wordbook of the Old Testament* (Chicago, IL: Moody Press, 1999, c1980), electronic ed., page 449.

coast of South America all the way up to the tropical areas of Peru and the Galápagos Islands.[12]

Ross provides another argument that betrays his *a priori* acceptance of uniformitarianism. Near the end of the Flood, Noah released some birds to help determine if the land was suitable for life yet. Ross states:

> At first, neither the raven nor the dove Noah released could fly far enough to find a landing place. A week later, when Noah sent the dove out again, it recovered a leaf from an olive tree. Olive trees do not grow at Earth's highest elevations, and yet this tree lived. We can reasonably assume that the *har* [Hebrew for *hills* or *mountains*] Noah finally saw were low-lying hills or foothills.[13]

This assumption is only reasonable if one assumes a local flood. This is circular reasoning. As the waters receded from the earth and the mountaintops became visible, it is certain that they were not snow-capped. The warm ocean water would have kept the land, which at the time consisted of mountain peaks, warm enough for plant life to grow. Perhaps Dr. Ross does not realize that Dr. Henry Morris and John Whitcomb already addressed this issue over 40 years ago in their seminal work *The Genesis Flood*.[14] They demonstrated that it would not be very difficult for an olive branch deposited near the surface of the sediments to have asexually reproduced to generate a new tree as the ground dried. This is a likely explanation for the source of the olive leaf carried by the dove (Gen. 8: 11).

Poetic Considerations . . . Again

As we saw in chapter 3, old-earth creationists have resorted to citing selected poetic sections of the Bible as justification for reinterpreting the clear meaning of the historical narratives of Genesis. This has been applied not only to the days of creation, but to the Flood

---

12. http://www.seaworld.org/animal-info/info-books/penguin/habitat-&-distribution.htm. Accessed May 17, 2007.
13. Ross, *The Genesis Question*, p. 146.
14. Henry Morris and John Whitcomb, *The Genesis Flood* (Philadelphia, PA: Presbyterian and Reformed Pub. Co., 1961).

as well. Old-earth creationist Steve Sarigianis wrote about Psalm 104, "Verses 5–9 describe the recently formed Earth, a period before creation of advanced life, when oceans completely covered the globe. . . . The Psalm then goes on to clearly state that water would *never again* completely cover the planet."[15]

By treating a Psalm of praise as if it were a creation account, Sarigianis is arguing that the Flood could not have been global. He has used poetry to override the clear meaning of Genesis 9:11. The proper hermeneutic is the reverse; Genesis 9:11 is the historic account of God's promise to never again flood the earth with water. Psalm 104:9 was written long after the Flood, and it reiterates God's promise that the flood waters will never return to flood the entire world.

The description of the great flood fits these verses better than creation. When we read Psalm 104:7, the description of the waters standing above the mountains reminds us of Genesis 7:20, which teaches that the "mountains were covered" by the Flood waters. The *Commentary Critical and Explanatory on the Whole Bible* by Jamieson, Fausset, and Brown (1871) states the following about Psalm 104:6–9:

> These verses rather describe the wonders of the flood than the creation (Genesis 7:19–20, 2 Peter 3:5–6). God's method of arresting the flood and making its waters subside is poetically called a "rebuke" (Psalm 76:6, Isaiah 50:2), and the process of the flood's subsiding by undulations among the hills and valleys is vividly described.[16]

Dr. John Whitcomb, a contemporary Bible scholar who has given much study to this matter, states:

> A second passage that sheds important light on the termination of the Flood is Psalm 104:6–9. Though it contains several figures of speech, the passage is clearly historical in its reference to the Flood. Note, for example, the statement of

---

15. S. Sarigianis, "Noah's Flood: A Bird's-Eye View," *Facts for Faith*, issue 10, 2002. <http://www.reasons.org/resources/fff/2002issue10/index.shtml>

16. <http://www.studylight.org/com/jfb/view.cgi?book=ps&chapter=104> Accessed May 30, 2007.

verse 6 — "the waters were standing above the mountains," and that of verse 9 — "Thou didst set a boundary that they may not pass over; that they may not return to cover the earth." The latter is obviously a reference to the Rainbow Covenant of Genesis 9, in which God assured mankind that there would *never again* be a universal Flood (cf. Isa. 54:9).[17]

Dr. Whitcomb rightly uses the historical account in Genesis to shed light on these poetic passages. In a very similar way, we must take the historical narrative of the crossing of the Red Sea in Exodus 14 as our basis for understanding the poetic song celebrating that event in Exodus 15. We would get some very erroneous ideas about the Exodus if we use chapter 15 to interpret chapter 14.[18]

Even if Psalm 104:6–9 were referring to events of the creation week, as some commentators suggest, these poetic passages cannot be used to override the clear teaching of Genesis that waters did cover "all the high hills under the whole heaven" (Gen. 7:19). The narratives tell us how to properly interpret the poetic imagery.

Misrepresenting the Other Side . . . Again

In chapter 4, we demonstrated that some old-earth creationists have resorted to straw-man arguments. Once the straw man is built, it is very easy to knock down. Misrepresenting the position of one's opponent may be effective, but is not a proper debating procedure — especially for Christians. We are followers of the One who called himself the Truth (John 14:6). As such, it is important for us to strive to accurately represent the position we are critiquing. Only when this is done can the reader make an honest and informed decision.

Unfortunately, straw-man arguments are common in Dr. Ross's books. While addressing the amount of water needed to cover the mountains in his book *The Genesis Question*, he wrote:

> Some global Flood proponents who acknowledge the problem of a grossly inadequate water supply propose that

---

17. J. Whitcomb, *The World that Perished* (Grand Rapids, MI: Baker Book House, 1988), p. 37, 40.
18. The same applies to Deborah's poetic song in Judges 6 commemorating her military victory historically recorded in Judges 5.

Earth's surface was "smoothed," or flattened, by the Flood, thus reducing the water requirement. More specifically, they claim that during the forty days and nights when the floodwaters rose, Earth's mountains radically eroded from their lofty heights of ten, fifteen, and even twenty thousand feet to just one or two thousand feet, perhaps less.[19]

It is not surprising that Ross does not provide any documentation for this statement, since we have never heard any young-earth creationist claim this. In fact, Ross has it entirely backward. Young-earth creationists do not believe the pre-Flood world had the lofty peaks that we see today. Also, the oceans were probably not as deep prior to the Flood. Ross claims that young-earthers believe these things were a result of the Flood. In reality, young-earthers believe the high mountains and the current depths of the oceans were produced in the recession phase of the Flood. As was discussed in the previous chapter, Psalm 104:8 (NASB) states, "The mountains rose; the valleys sank down."

In his book *A Matter of Days*, Ross includes a chapter entitled "Young Earth Darwinism." He writes:

Young-earth creationist leaders' views on the Fall (Adam and Eve's original sin) and on the Genesis Flood drive them — knowingly or not — into the surprising corner of belief in ultraefficient biological evolution.[20]

This is another example of misrepresenting the young-earth side. What makes this case particularly indicting is that Dr. Kent Hovind had previously explained this to Dr. Ross during their debate on the *John Ankerberg Show*. Young-earth creationists do not believe in particles-to-people biological evolution at all. What Ross is referring to is the belief that every dog observed in the world today descended from two dogs that were on board Noah's ark and that this diversification of wild and domestic dogs happened quite rapidly (in about 4,000 years since the Flood). However, the concept of dogs turning into dogs is not evolution. This process of diversification within the original created kinds

19. Ross, *The Genesis Question*.
20. Ross, *A Matter of Days*, p. 122.

or from the kinds that came off the ark has been frequently and thoroughly explained by young-earth creationists,[21] so Ross really ought to know better than to claim it has anything to do with Darwinian evolution in the molecules-to-man sense.

Young-earthers do not have a problem with natural selection. But natural selection is very different from evolution, though Darwin popularized it as the means by which he believed evolution occurred. It may come as a surprise to most people, but Darwin did not discover natural selection. A creationist, Edward Blyth, discussed the idea 24 years before Darwin published *Origin of Species*. Although he did not use the term, Blyth rightly understood that natural selection is a conservative process, allowing the created kinds to adapt to changing environments, food supplies, etc., but not changing one kind into a different kind. Further research has demonstrated that natural selection can only act upon genetic information already present. It can never add any new information. But Darwinian evolution would require that organisms somehow gain new (previously non-existent) genetic information (new instructions in their DNA) in order to evolve from single-celled organisms to people. Overall, natural selection results in a net *loss* of information; it goes in the "wrong direction." As such, it has nothing to do with evolution in the Darwinian sense of the term. Ross also knows that most of the domestic breeds of dog in the world today are the result of artificial selection (humans choosing which animals will mate to produce a desired trait in the offspring) over the past few centuries.

This straw-man attack is nothing more than an attempt to make the young-earth position appear to contradict itself. Young-earthers do not accept Darwinian evolution; however, in this argument, we are portrayed as accepting an "ultraefficient" form of it. Nothing could be further from the truth. The fact of the matter is that we have no problem with natural selection and have produced numerous resources explaining our position. (See Appendix F for a recommended list of books on the scientific aspects of the debate.) Natural selection actually confirms biblical creation; the gradual loss of information is what we would expect in a cursed, fallen world.

---

21. See "Speedy Species Surprise" at http://www.answersingenesis.org/creation/v23/i2/speciation.asp. Accessed May 30, 2007.

Conclusions

We have seen that the local flood arguments simply do not stand up to scrutiny. The language of the Genesis account makes it abundantly clear that the Flood waters covered all the high hills under the whole heavens. Local flood proponents have argued for a limited extent of sin. They have tried redefining words and phrases. They have attempted to use poetic sections to override the historical account in Genesis. When all else fails, they sometimes misrepresent their opponents' position. However, we have seen that these tactics are neither biblically nor logically sound. Yet, old-earth creationists must hold to a local flood, because a global flood "washes away" the supposed evidence for an old earth. The rock record is exactly what we would expect from a year-long, global, catastrophic flood. If the majority of fossils and sedimentary rock layers were deposited in the worldwide flood, then they cannot have been deposited over millions of years. The biblical evidence for the global flood is further strong confirmation that the world is young.

Chapter 7

Prosecution — The Philosophy and Correct Application of Science

At this point, we have established that the Bible unequivocally teaches a "young" earth. In other words, God created the universe and the earth in six ordinary days, roughly 6,000 years ago. But what do the scientific dating methods indicate?

In this chapter we will examine the nature and role of science, as well as the ability and limitations of scientific dating methods. It is crucial that we have a proper understanding of how science works, and the underlying philosophy and assumptions involved in any age-dating method before any accurate age estimates can be made. We will then apply proper scientific techniques to the evidence. We will find that the scientific evidence confirms the biblical age of the earth of several thousand years.

The Bible First

The Bible must come first in our quest for knowledge; it is superior to other sources of information, including knowledge gained from the natural sciences. This must be the case because other sources of knowledge *presuppose* the Bible. In other words, in order for us to gain knowledge about anything in the universe through any means (including scientific analysis), we would have to *already* assume that the Bible is true. People do not often realize this, so let's briefly explore this idea.

In order for science to be possible, what things must be true?[1] What are the things that scientists assume (presuppose) before any investigation of evidence? Scientists presuppose that the universe obeys logical, rational laws, and that the human mind is able to discover and understand these laws and make predictions about how the universe will be in the future. Without these assumptions, science would be impossible. Yet, these assumptions are exactly what we would expect from the Bible. God is rational and upholds the universe in a logical, orderly fashion — which we call the "laws of nature." And since God made our minds to be able to function in this universe (and since we are made in God's image), it stands to reason that our minds would have the ability to discover truths about the universe.

But without the Bible, we wouldn't have justification for these truths. This isn't to say that unbelievers cannot do science; they can. The non-Christian also assumes a rational, orderly universe, and a rational mind that can understand the universe. But the non-Christian cannot *justify* these concepts within his own worldview; he cannot account for what he is doing. Science cannot be rationally used to override the plain teaching of the Bible, because the plain teaching of the Bible is required in order for science to be possible.

Furthermore, since the Bible has never been wrong about anything, and since it is the very Word of the One who knows everything, we must place our confidence in the Bible above all other sources of information. Many old-earth creationists do not accept this principle. Instead, they have a tendency to put the Bible at the same level (in principle) or below the level (in practice) of the latest secular scientific theories. This is rationalized under the premise that since God made the universe, nature must be as truthful as the Bible. Old-earth creationists

---

1. These kinds of questions concerning the preconditions of intelligibility are a powerful way of defending the Christian worldview. The late Christian philosopher Dr. Greg Bahnsen specialized in this kind of apologetic. A student of Dr. Cornelius Van Till, Dr. Bahnsen was known as "the man atheists most feared" due to his ability to destroy non-Christian worldviews (especially atheism) on the basis of preconditions of intelligibility.

will sometimes say it like this: "The record of nature must be just as perfect, and reliable and truthful as the 66 books of the Bible that is part of the Word of God."[2] As mentioned earlier, Dr. Hugh Ross has said, "The facts of nature may be likened to a sixty-seventh book of the Bible."[3]

> **Worldview** – *a person's underlying philosophy and assumptions about how the world works.*

However, there is a fundamental error with this reasoning. Nature is not propositional truth. Propositional truth is a statement or sequence of statements that are true. However, nature is not comprised of statements! Therefore, nature cannot be true or false; it simply is. If I held up a rock and asked someone to evaluate whether it was true or false, this would make no sense. True and false apply to statements. If I made a statement about the rock ("This rock exists"), then we could evaluate the statement as true, but not the rock itself. Likewise, when scientists make statements about nature, we can evaluate those statements as true or false, but not nature itself.

In fact, the "record of nature" is somewhat misnamed because a record is an account in writing, whereas nature is not written. Again, nature is not propositional truth. On the other hand, the Bible is propositional truth. It is a sequence of statements, and all the statements that are affirmed in the Bible are true. In a sense, the Bible is the "record of nature" since it records the creation of the universe and many of the major events of history. It is simply false when old-earth creationists talk of fossils and rocks as a "record of nature" that is supposedly comparable to the Bible.

This isn't to say that we cannot learn anything from nature. When evidence from the natural world is properly interpreted, it can provide a wealth of information. However, the way in which such evidence is interpreted depends largely on what a person already believes about the world. Most people are unaware of how significantly a worldview affects one's interpretation of data. This is an important principle, and we will revisit this in detail later. For now, it is sufficient to say that the

---

2. H. Ross, Toccoa Falls College, Staley Lecture Series, March 1997.
3. H. Ross, *Creation and Time: A Biblical and Scientific Perspective on the Creation-Date Controversy*, (Wheaton, IL: NavPress, 1994), p. 56

conclusions scientists draw from data are very strongly influenced by their beliefs. Science is not nearly as objective as many people believe it to be.

There are several problems with treating scientific theories about nature as if they were at the same level as Scripture. First, as mentioned in chapter 4, nature is cursed (Rom. 8; Gen. 3), whereas the Bible is not. This instantly places the Bible in a higher position.

Second, scientific theories are not nature, rather they are statements made by men about nature. As such, they are fallible, whereas the Bible is not. It is true that we can misunderstand the Bible and we can also misunderstand scientific claims. However, we must remember that the Bible is never wrong, whereas scientific claims sometimes are.

Third, the way in which we interpret nature is strongly dependent on what we believe about the world. In order to do science at all, we must accept some of the truths of the Bible. As such, the Bible is actually the foundation of science.

This is not to say that we should never trust scientific theories; many of them are very well established. However, when there is a conflict between the ideas of men and the Word of God, the Bible must be considered our ultimate authority, because scientists can and have made mistakes. (It happens a lot — take it from me!) But God knows everything and never errs nor lies. So, unlike human wisdom, the Bible is an infallible source of information. Since the Bible teaches a young earth, we can know for certain that the earth is young.

This really should be enough for a Bible-believing Christian. Sadly, it's been our experience that few professing Christians really believe the Bible in its entirety. They may believe that the Bible has moral value and they may even believe much of biblical history — such as the death and resurrection of Christ. However, when secular scientists tell them that we know the world is billions of years old, they crumble. Many Christians simply will not believe the history recorded in Genesis 1, no matter how clear the text is, because they place more faith in men than in God. They will either reject Genesis outright, or worse, they will "reinterpret" the Bible to match the secular notion of billions of years. However, when someone "reinterprets" the clear meaning of the words to accommodate outside notions, it simply means he does not believe the words.

"Reinterpreting" = not believing the text

However, many of the evidential old-earth arguments are really nothing more than unbiblical, faulty philosophy disguised as science. When we understand the role of science, and apply it properly, we will find that it supports the biblical time scale. We offer these two chapters to help people understand that when scientific evidence is correctly interpreted, it will confirm what the Bible teaches.

The Nature of Science

The word "science" comes from the Latin *scientia*, which means "knowledge." So, in its broadest sense, science is what we *know*. Under this definition, all historic events, including all the events recorded in the Bible, fall within the realm of science.

Today, many dictionaries will define science as knowledge that has been gained through observation and experimentation. This is the most common definition today and it is more restrictive than the original meaning. For example, we do know some things that fall outside the modern definition of science. Recorded history is one example. We know that Abraham Lincoln became president of the United States. We know this, but not because we have observed it, or confirmed it by experimentation; rather, we know it because we have reliable historical records.

Operational Science and Origins Science

Since science relies on observation and experimentation, it is well suited for describing and quantifying how the universe operates today. To be clear, we'll call this kind of study "operational science." Operational science would include such branches as physics, chemistry, and biology. For example, by observing how things fall, and by performing controlled experiments, we can deduce the formula for gravity, as Isaac Newton did. This formula, along with other laws of physics, can then be used to make predictions about the future — such as the positions of the planets next year. For the most part, physics, chemistry, and biology describe the way the world operates today, and therefore fall under the scope of operational science.

The topics of creation, evolution, and the age of the earth do not fall under the category of operational science. These issues pertain to the past — how and when the universe came into existence. This is not something that can be answered directly by observation and experimentation. That's not to say that the methods and processes of operational science cannot shed light on these issues. Clearly, scientific methods can help inform our understanding of the past. However, since the past is gone, it cannot be observed, nor can we experiment on it.

The above statement may seem obvious, but many people do not really grasp this concept. In fact, many have objected to this concept by saying, "But a fossil is a piece of the past." This objection just is not true. A fossil is a piece of the present; otherwise we would not have it! We could certainly make some guesses about how and when the fossil formed in the past. But, could operational science ever prove these guesses to be true? No. At best, operational science could establish that fossils can be formed in a certain way today. For example, by creating fossils in a laboratory, we know that they can form very quickly under the right conditions. But operational science could never prove for certain how a particular fossil formed if that fossil's formation was not observed. Past events are not accessible to operational science because they cannot be observed or experimented upon.

Of course, there is nothing wrong with making a reasonable conjecture about how a fossil formed by drawing on the observations and experiments of operational science. For example, operational science tells us that fossils and rock layers can form very quickly under flood conditions. It is therefore reasonable to conjecture that many of the fossils and rock layers of the earth were formed during a particularly massive flood. Applying scientific techniques of the present to answer a question about the past is called "origins science." Note that some branches of study, such as astronomy and geology, include both operational and origins science.

Origins science is an attempt to answer a *history* question using science. Radiometric dating is one example. The radioactive elements contained in a certain rock are measured (in the present: this is the *science* part — it is testable and repeatable), and then (along with certain assumptions that we will discuss below) an estimation is made about how long ago the rock formed. In principle, there is no reason why such a guess cannot be made. However, origins science is much less certain than operational science, because it is difficult to ever prove or disprove the conclusions. How do we really know for certain how long ago the rock formed? Any "scientific" age estimate is really just an educated guess, and in most cases it is impossible to know with any certainty whether that guess is actually correct. We should also understand that questions of age and history are best answered by consulting a history book, if one is available.

Consider the following facetious example. Suppose two students are asked to find out when World War I started. This is obviously a history question. The first student consults several history books written around the time and finds that they generally agree on the date. He concludes that it began in A.D. 1914. The second student puts on his white lab coat, and gathers a number of chemicals, beakers, and DNA samples, and begins experimentation in a laboratory. After several weeks, he concludes from his experiments that World War I began 3.7 million years ago. Which student would you be more inclined to believe? What if the second student actually held a PhD in geology and had just won a Nobel Prize? Would this change your mind?

Hopefully, you would dismiss the 3.7-million-year date as absurd since recorded history indicates precisely when the war began. Even without knowing the details, we can conclude that the second student was mistaken. His education and accomplishments are irrelevant. It would be simply absurd to reject recorded history in favor of guesswork — even "scientific" guesswork. And yet this is precisely what many people do when it comes to the age of the earth. When we ask about the age of something, we are not asking a science question, but rather a history question. We are asking, "At what point in the past did something come into existence?" Why is it that when it comes to the age of the earth, people reject the recorded history of the Bible in favor of "scientific" guesswork? It seems that many Christians do not have any real confidence in the Bible.

The Bible as a Starting Point for Science

Many times, unbelievers will ask a Christian to leave the Bible out of the discussion when talking about the age of the earth or evolution. The foolish response would be to accept these terms, say okay, and then proceed to throw science evidences at the unbeliever without the Bible. And sadly, this is what many Christians do. This approach is generally futile.

It tends to be ineffective because the unbeliever does not have the correct worldview to properly interpret the evidence. The wise Christian never abandons the Word of God — he must challenge the assumptions of the unbeliever rather than accept them! Proverbs 26:4 states, "Do not answer a fool according to his folly, Lest you also be like him."[4]

By this, we are not implying that all unbelievers are fools, but it is most certainly "folly" to start with the assumption that the Bible is not true or is irrelevant to origins. Why? Because the Bible is true and is very relevant to origins, considering it is the Word of a perfect God who has always been there and created everything. Why would we start with an assumption that is false?

Proverbs 26:5 states, "Answer a fool according to his folly, Lest he be wise in his own eyes." Some people think that this verse contradicts verse 4, but they are mistaken. Verses 4 and 5 together do not form a contradiction; they form a strategy. We do not accept the erroneous, unbiblical assumptions of the unbeliever or we would be like him (verse 4). However, we can and should, for the sake of argument, show where his erroneous assumptions would lead if they were true. In

4. New American Standard, 1977.

other words, we show how the unbeliever's faulty assumptions lead to a ridiculous conclusion that he does not accept. This will demonstrate that he cannot be "wise" for starting with such fallacious assumptions (verse 5). This may sound very abstract, so we will illustrate it with the following example.

An unbeliever might say, "I'm an evolutionist; your view is unscientific because you believe that God created the universe. If you're going to prove that evolution is false then you have to use the laws of science only." Rather than buying into this premise, we challenge it (Prov. 26:4). We might say, "Why do you think a belief in God is 'unscientific'? This isn't true; in fact, it is because God exists that science is possible. Think about it: the reason the universe is orderly and logical is because a logical God has imposed order on His creation. It's because God created our minds that we are able to discover the laws of science that He created." We then respectfully show the inconsistency in the unbeliever's thinking (Prov. 26:5). "If the universe were just an accident as you believe, then why should it obey orderly principles? Why should there be laws if there is no Lawgiver? You have accepted the biblical principle of an orderly, logical universe, while simultaneously denying the God who makes such order possible."

This same kind of approach can be used on old-earth creationists. We will show that they accept secular, anti-biblical assumptions while simultaneously claiming to believe the Bible. Such inconsistencies are common in old-earth creationism. In the next few sections, we will compare and contrast the biblical and secular philosophies of science. Note that, for the most part, old-earth creationists embrace the secular assumptions of science rather than the biblical ones. So, we are really contrasting the young earther's biblical assumptions with the old earther's secular assumptions.

The Biblical Axioms of Science

The consistent Christian approaches science from the following perspective. Since God created the universe, and since God is logical, we expect the universe to be logical. We expect it to obey rational laws, since God is the ultimate Lawgiver. Since God created our minds, and has given us stewardship of the earth (Gen. 1:26, 28), we expect to be able to understand, to some degree, how the world works. Since God is the omnipresent sustainer of all things, and since He does not change, it makes sense that God would not arbitrarily change the way He sustains the universe. Granted, there have been times when God has acted in an extraordinary way to accomplish an extraordinary purpose. But the fact that God normally upholds the universe in a logical and quantifiable way is what the Christian would expect. The laws of nature are descriptions of the logical, consistent way that the Lord sustains the universe. The fact that these laws apply throughout space and do not vary with time is a reflection of God's omnipresent and consistent nature.

Interestingly, secular scientists also embrace the above biblical principles of science, although they deny the biblical basis for these principles. That is to say, secular scientists agree that the universe is logical and orderly, that it obeys natural laws, that the mind is able to understand much of the universe, and that the laws of nature are constant with time and space. Yet, they would have no logical reason to believe these things if the Bible were not true. This is a very blatant inconsistency in secular thinking, and so we will explore this in greater detail later.

However, there are some additional biblical assumptions of science that are embraced by the consistent Christian but are usually rejected by the secular scientist. For one, Christians have a supernatural worldview. That is, we allow for miracles. In fact, we insist on them. Since God is beyond the universe that He created, we know that He is able to work outside natural law, and according to the Bible, He occasionally does. We could define a "natural law" as a "description of the way God normally upholds the universe." A miracle would occur when God acts in an unusual way to accomplish an extraordinary purpose. The resurrection of Christ would be one example. God does not normally raise the dead today.

Another biblical axiom is that God created the universe supernaturally. During the creation week, God was acting in a way that He does not today. God was speaking into existence new things — the land, the plants, the sun, the moon, the stars, and the animals. God also created Adam from the dust of the earth, and Eve from Adam's side. God is not doing these things today and the Bible specifically tells us this. It states that God ended His work of creation by the seventh day (Gen. 2:2). Therefore, the consistent Christian does not expect that the laws of nature (which describe how God upholds the world today) can properly describe how God created the world.

Today, for example, we have the law of conservation of energy and mass, which states that no new energy or mass can come into existence. This law was obviously not in effect (at least in its present form) during the creation week; new energy and mass were coming into existence at God's command. Likewise, the consistent Christian expects that God will again act in a supernatural way when He brings an end to this world and creates a new heaven and earth. Biblical miracles such as the resurrection of Christ and the creation of the universe are historical facts. They are true but are largely beyond the scope of operational science.

One must understand that the way God created the universe is not the same as the way He maintains the universe today. This is absolutely clear from the Bible. Secular scientists deny this principle, since they deny biblical creation. They are forced to assume (not because of facts, but because of their philosophical bias) that the creation of the universe was a natural event. They expect that the processes that formed the universe are the same as those that are acting within the universe today. Even though this is unbiblical, this secular assumption is also largely embraced by old-earth creationists, as will be shown in the next chapter.

One last biblical axiom has to do with the geological impact of the Flood. After the Flood, God promised to never again send such a devastating Flood of waters upon the earth (Gen. 8:21, 9:11). So, we can infer from Scripture that the Flood was the most geologically significant event since creation. Psalm 104:8 suggests that mountains rose and valleys sank during this catastrophe. Therefore, we would expect that many of earth's geologic features, such as mountains, canyons, volcanoes, and rock layers were shaped rapidly during and soon after the worldwide flood.

Secular Assumptions in Science

We have seen that most secular scientists use a number of biblical assumptions when doing science. They assume (just as a Christian does) that the universe obeys natural laws, that these laws do not change with time or space, and that the human mind is capable of understanding the laws of nature, etc. However, the secular scientist has no logical reason to believe these things if the universe were merely an accident. He might argue that he uses these assumptions because they work — they make science possible. But that does not explain why they are true, whereas the Bible does explain this.

Because of his denial of Scripture, the secular scientist has several assumptions that differ from the Christian's perspective. These assumptions deal largely with origins science rather than operational science. This explains why Christians and non-Christians largely agree on matters of operational science; that is, we agree on how the universe works today. However, we disagree about the past because the secular scientists make a number of philosophical assumptions that are unbiblical and unfounded. The two most obvious are *naturalism* and *uniformitarianism*.

Naturalism is the belief that nature is all that exists. A naturalist does not believe in miracles. He believes that everything that happens or has ever happened has occurred within the laws of nature. This even includes the origin of nature. The secular scientist assumes that everything that exists is the result of the laws of nature working over time. Curiously, a number of secular scientists do believe in God, or some version of a supreme being. However, they seem to regard this as irrelevant to their studies. It is as if they intentionally pretend that "nature is all that there is" when in fact they believe that to be false. Naturalism has become the *modus operandi* of the secular scientist in our day. It is the guiding principle to which virtually all secular scientists adhere. Yet, it is false.

> *Naturalism — the belief that nature is all that exists. Inherent in this belief is the denial of miracles.*

If naturalism were true, it would be impossible to prove anything.[5] Proofs involve use of the laws of logic, such as the law of non-contradiction, which says that you can't have A, and not-A at the same

---

5. This was brilliantly demonstrated by Christian philosopher Dr. Greg Bahnsen in the "Great Debate" on the existence of God. In this debate, Dr. Bahnsen showed that his opponent (atheist Gordon Stein) could not even make sense of the debate itself without presupposing the biblical God.

time and in the same relationship. The laws of logic are not part of nature. They are not part of the physical universe. You can't stub your toe on a law of logic. So, if nature (the physical universe) is all that exists and if laws of logic are not part of nature, then they can't exist. But they are required for rational reasoning. So, the naturalist view is actually self-refuting. If it were true, it would be impossible to reason. Yet naturalism is what secular scientists use as the foundation for their thinking. We will show why this explains many of the incorrect conclusions drawn by secular scientists, such as evolution and an old earth.

Uniformitarianism is the belief that nature is uniform. This term can be used in more than one way, so let's expand on this. First, uniformitarianism can simply mean that the laws of nature do not arbitrarily change with time. Of course, this is true. It is a biblical principle that God has maintained the universe consistently since its creation.[6] We part company with secular scientists when they assume that the laws of nature have always applied — even to the origin of the universe and life. We do this because the Bible teaches that God created the universe and life supernaturally.

More frequently, the term *uniformitarianism* is the assumption that rates have always been generally the same as they are today.[7] This is summed up in the phrase "the present is the key to the past." Secular scientists observe that canyons are deepening, and some mountains are slowly lifting today. They assume that these present rates have been more or less constant throughout time. If that were the case, then it would take a very long time for mountains and canyons to form. Uniformitarianism assumes that the major geologic features of earth

---

6. Though, at the Fall, God apparently removed some of His sustaining power. This was certainly a change — but not an arbitrary one. God had an important reason for doing this.

7. Uniformitarianism doesn't necessarily mean that we assume a given rate itself is necessarily constant, only that the *trend* we see today has always applied. For example, radioactive decay is not *constant*; it is an exponential decay (it happens slower as the source material is depleted). So the uniformitarianism assumption in this case is that radioactive decay has *always been* an exponential decay and that the "decay constant" (a mathematical term describing the "steepness" of the exponential decay curve) has never changed. Another example is the recession of the moon; this rate is not constant — it goes as the sixth power of distance. So the uniformitarian assumption is that this has always been the case.

were formed gradually over vast periods of time by the slow and gradual processes we observe happening today. Since we do not observe a worldwide flood today, this event is dismissed out-of-hand by the uniformitarian scientist.

We are not suggesting that it is always unbiblical and wrong to assume that a particular process has been constant throughout time. For example, we believe the orbit of earth around the sun has remained about the same since God created the sun on the fourth day. However, we should always have a good, cogent reason for making such an assumption on a case-by-case basis. In addition, we certainly would not assume a rate is constant when we have good biblical reasons to believe otherwise. For example, there are certainly some universal biblical events that would have affected the rates at which some things occur. The global flood killed people and animals at a much greater rate than is happening today. So our disagreement with secular scientists is not that rates are never constant, but rather that (1) secular scientists have a tendency to arbitrarily assume that such rates are generally constant, and (2) that secular scientists ignore biblical events, such as creation and the Flood, that would most certainly affect the rates of various physical processes. The present is not the key to the past. The biblically minded person should realize that the reverse is true: the Bible (which tells us about the *past*) is the key to (understanding) the *present*.

It is clear that a belief in naturalism and uniformitarianism would lead to vastly inflated estimated ages for the earth and its various features. If we incorrectly assumed that the earth had formed by natural processes, then we would incorrectly conclude that it took a great deal of time for the earth to cool from the molten blob from which it allegedly formed. If we incorrectly assumed that there was no worldwide flood to push up mountains and form canyons, then we would incorrectly conclude that it took vast ages for these features to form at today's rates. These conclusions are not irrational; they follow logically from the starting assumptions. However, the starting assumptions are wrong — and consequently, so are the conclusions! We will now examine how these assumptions and others adversely affect the unbeliever's estimates of the age of the earth.

The Assumptions of Age-dating Methods

Recall that questions of age are not "science" questions but history questions, since they ask when in the past something happened. Age is not a substance that can be measured in the present by scientific processes. Age-dating methods are applied to a process — where something changes to something else at a known rate, such as the radioactive decay of substances in a rock. By extrapolating backward, one can estimate when the process began. There are several assumptions involved in this process that cast serious doubts on such methods.

It has been our experience that very few people really understand the assumptions involved in science — especially those of the age-dating methods of origins science. There are three significant assumptions involved in almost all age-dating techniques. These are the constancy of rates, the initial conditions of the system, and the assumption that the system is "closed" (which means that no material from the system is exchanged with the outside world). In this text, we will deal primarily with the first two assumptions. These assumptions tie in very strongly with the assumptions of naturalism and uniformitarianism.

Here is an example to illustrate these assumptions. Suppose a friend decided to pay us a surprise visit one day. We have not seen him for a while because he moved to a town 500 miles away several years ago. We notice that he is moving at 50 miles per hour as he arrives. We wonder how long ago he began his trip. This is a history question. To travel 500 miles at 50 miles per hour would take ten hours. So we conclude he began his journey ten hours ago. Of course, this may not be accurate because we have employed the above assumptions, which may not be true. He may have been traveling faster than 50 miles per hour for most of the trip, only slowing down for the last leg. In this case, our age estimate would be too high. We have assumed the *constancy of rates*, when the rate was not constant.

We have also made another assumption. It may be that he no longer lives in that city 500 miles away but now lives in a town that is only 50 miles away. So even if his rate really were constant, it would only take him one hour to arrive rather than ten. In this case, we have assumed the incorrect initial conditions, and this leads us to a vastly inflated age estimate.

Secular Assumptions and the Age of the Earth

Since the majority of secular scientists believe in naturalism and uniformitarianism, this causes them to make incorrect assumptions about the initial conditions and constancy of rates of various earth processes. These faulty assumptions lead to inflated estimates for the age of the earth. Here is a real-world example to illustrate this concept.

Today it is estimated that the Grand Canyon is eroding at a rate of 168 million tons per year.[8] When we factor in the average density of material (2.0 g/cm^3), this works out to a volume of 0.018 cubic miles per year of sediment that is removed. The Grand Canyon itself is just under 1,000 cubic miles in volume. If we divide 1,000 by 0.018, we find that it would take over 50,000 years[9] for the Colorado River to remove enough material to form the Grand Canyon at today's rate of erosion.

Notice the assumptions that have gone into this estimation. One assumption would be the starting conditions. We have assumed that there was not a canyon there to begin with — it really was cut out of pre-existing rock. This is a pretty safe assumption since the rock layers are mostly sedimentary rocks — the kind laid down by water. Most people would agree that the earth was not created with a Grand Canyon already there; so the Christian and non-Christian agree on the starting conditions in this case.

What about the rate of erosion? Have we made an unwarranted assumption here? Is it possible that the rate at which water cuts the canyon was faster in the past? Certainly! We know from Scripture that there was once a worldwide flood that killed all air-breathing land animals[10] and people except those on the ark (Gen. 7:21–23). Such a catastrophic event would lay down many successive layers of sediment, trapping the remains of animals killed during the Flood. We would

---

8. S. Austin et al., *Grand Canyon: Monument to Catastrophe* (Santee, CA: Institute for Creation Research, 1994), p. 87

9. Most secular geologists believe that the Grand Canyon is *millions* of years old. But as we can see, this is difficult to support even if we assume today's slow and gradual rate of erosion.

10. Specifically, those land animals which have the "breath of life" died. The Hebrew phrase implies that this is a subclass of animals, possibly referring primarily to vertebrate animals (though we would not be dogmatic on this point).

expect to find layers of rocks containing fossils all around the world — and this is exactly what we do find. The walls of the Grand Canyon are made of these fossil-bearing sedimentary rock layers. So the canyon formed after the Flood.

Since all the land on earth was covered with water (Gen. 7:17), the amount of water that rushed into the oceans after the Flood would have been staggering! Such a massive quantity of water would have certainly cut canyons quickly. We know that such things can happen, because we have recently observed smaller canyons forming in a matter of days from massive flooding.

A consistent Christian would conclude that most of the Grand Canyon must have formed rapidly by catastrophic amounts of water and mud shortly after the worldwide flood. But since the unbeliever adheres to uniformitarianism, he denies the biblical flood, and consequently his estimated age of the Grand Canyon is far too old. Faulty starting assumptions have resulted in faulty conclusions. We will examine more of these kinds of arguments in the next chapter.

Whenever we come across any age-dating technique, we need to think about what assumptions have gone into it. When it comes to estimating the age of something, the Christian should always examine the assumptions about initial conditions, the constancy of rates, and whether the system was closed. This is not to say that a creationist would always disagree with the assumptions of a particular age estimate. Sometimes we have good reasons to think that certain rates really have been essentially constant; however, we do not arbitrarily assume that this is so. Moreover, we certainly do not assume constancy of rates when we have good biblical reasons to believe otherwise, such as the rapid changes in earth's topography caused by the worldwide flood.

Don't Answer, Answer

In the spirit of Proverbs 26:4, we refuse to accept the erroneous and unbiblical philosophies of uniformitarianism and naturalism. These doctrines have caused unbelievers to make incorrect assumptions about initial conditions and constancy of rates. In fact, virtually all old-earth arguments assume these false philosophies. Clearly, we cannot accept the conclusions of age estimates that are based on faulty starting assumptions. Unfortunately, old-earth creationists generally do accept such arguments. In some cases, they may not have realized the assumptions from which such estimates are derived.

However, in the spirit of Proverbs 26:5, we can, for the sake of argument, show how the secular assumptions of naturalism and uniformitarianism would lead to logical inconsistencies. When creationists talk about scientific evidence that confirms the biblical age of the earth, this is usually how the topic is approached. For the sake of argument, we will assume naturalism (nature is all that there is) and uniformitarianism (rates are generally constant — no worldwide flood) in the following examples. Then we will show how the logical conclusions still contradict the notion of billions of years.[11]

Science Confirms a Young Earth

Rivers are constantly removing small fractions of salt from the land and transporting it to the ocean. The rate at which this happens has been measured. The salt added to the ocean by all the rivers in the world is about 450 million tons per year.[12] The water at the ocean's surface is constantly evaporating and then falls as rain, which collects in rivers, completing the cycle. The salt does not evaporate and only a fraction (27 percent is a generous upper limit) of the salt added to the ocean every year can be removed (by salt sprays and a handful of other processes). As a consequence, the ocean gets saltier every year by at least 330 million tons.

Assuming uniformitarianism (that this trend has been more-or-less constant throughout time), we can extrapolate backward to figure out when the ocean was entirely fresh water. In fact, just to be generous to the old-earth supporters, we will use a "worst-case scenario" rate even larger than today's rate. When we do the calculation, the answer we get is that the oceans cannot be older than 62 million years. Note that we have also assumed the "worst-case scenario" initial conditions; we have assumed the ocean had no salt in it at all when it was first created. If

---

11. Henry Morris listed 68 of these processes in Appendix 5 of *The Defender's Study Bible* (Grand Rapids, MI: World Publishing, 1995), p. 1505–1508.

12. S.A. Austin and D.R. Humphreys, "The Sea's Missing Salt: A Dilemma for Evolutionists," Proceedings of the 2nd International Conference on Creationism, Vol. II, Creation Science Fellowship 1991.

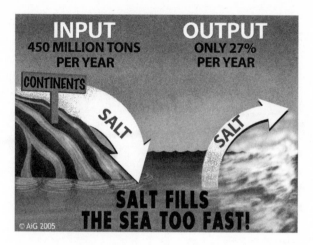

the ocean did have salt in it at its beginning, then the true age must be considerably less than 62 million years.

If we used today's rates, we would get 38 million years. These numbers may sound high, since they are much higher than 6,000 years, but evolutionists and other old-earth supporters believe that the oceans are three billion years old — 50 times older than our upper limit estimate. Yet, when we use their starting assumptions, we find that this cannot be true. The old-earth belief is inconsistent with its own assumptions.

Likewise, rivers also carry sediment from the continents into the oceans. This mud accumulates on the ocean floor. The rate at which this occurs is about 20 billion tons per year. The only significant way to remove such mud is thought to be subduction (plate tectonics), but this could only remove a maximum of one billion tons per year at current rates. The rest just accumulates.

How long would it take to get the current amount of mud in the oceans? Assuming uniformitarianism (no worldwide flood), and "worst-case scenario" initial conditions (we assume there was no mud at all to begin with), it would take 12 million years to get the present amount of mud. So even when we intentionally ignore the effects of a global flood (which would deposit a great deal of mud very rapidly) we still find that the oceans cannot be 3 billion years old, as taught by old-earthers.

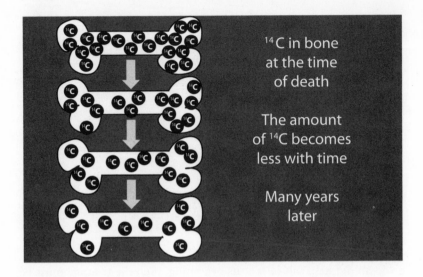

^{14}C in bone at the time of death

The amount of ^{14}C becomes less with time

Many years later

Many people have heard of carbon dating. Without being overly technical, it is sufficient to say that carbon dating is based on the process of Carbon-14 (C-14) changing to nitrogen.

This process happens at a known rate. By measuring the current amount of C-14 in a dead organism and by extrapolating backward, scientists can estimate when it died. As with virtually all age-dating methods, this technique assumes certain initial conditions and it assumes that the rate at which C-14 decays is constant.[13]

The problem for old earth supporters is that C-14 *always* gives "young" age estimates (a few thousand years) — even on things like coal beds that are supposedly millions of years old. At its current decay rate, C-14 simply cannot last even one million years. Yet, C-14 has been found in coal that is supposedly millions of years old and even in diamonds that are allegedly more than a *billion* years old.[14] Since diamonds are the hardest known substance, there is essentially no chance of contamination from the outside. So this is very compelling evidence that the earth is only thousands of years old.

---

13. To be precise, the uniformitarian assumption in this case is that the exponential decay constant does not change with time.
14. L. Vardiman, A.A. Snelling, and E.F. Chaffin, *Radioisotopes and the Age of the Earth Vol. II* (Santee, CA: Institute for Creation Research, 2005), p. 609.

Human population growth is another example. Starting with one man and one woman and using today's growth rate, it would take less than 2,000 years to get all the people on earth. Of course, even the strictest uniformitarian would have to grant that the growth rate was slightly less in the past because of famines, disease, higher infant mortality rate, etc. Even if we use a much lower growth rate, we still find that human beings have only been around for a few thousand years, which is much less than evolutionists and old-earth supporters assume. In order to be compatible with the secular time-line, the growth rate would have to be extremely different from today's rates, which is certainly incompatible with uniformitarianism. In fact, the growth rate would have to be essentially zero for hundreds of thousands of years. Of course, it is absurd to think that earth's population remained constant for such a long time.

In the above examples, we have used the same secular assumptions of naturalism and uniformitarianism employed by the old-earthers and have shown how these lead to an inconsistency. In many cases, the evidence is simply inconsistent with an old earth — even when secular assumptions are used. Of course, if we use our own Bible-based starting assumptions, there is no problem. We assume that the universe was supernaturally created. We assume that the world was created fully functional from the beginning and was similar in many respects to the way it is today[15] (with some important differences, of course), because the Bible indicates this. We assume that a worldwide flood is responsible for much of earth's topography today, since this is a logical inference from the Word of God. These starting assumptions are very consistent with scientific observations. Yet when we start with secular, old-earth assumptions, we find that such assumptions lead to inconsistencies.

The scientific case for a young earth is very strong. In the next chapter, we will examine scientific arguments that supposedly support an old earth.

---

15. This is to say that there were stars, galaxies, plants, and animals present right at the end of the first week.

Chapter 8

Defense — "Scientific" Arguments

We have commonly heard scientific-sounding arguments that the earth and universe are many billions of years old. We are told that radiometric dating shows that certain rocks formed billions of years ago. We are told that starlight from distant galaxies takes billions of years to arrive on earth. But do these arguments stand up to scrutiny? In this chapter, we will examine the most common scientific arguments for an old earth. We will find that in all cases the old-earth arguments are based on faulty, secular assumptions or faulty reasoning.

Biblical vs. Secular Assumptions

In the last chapter, we examined the nature of scientific dating techniques. Such techniques inevitably depend on a number of assumptions about the past. These assumptions include the initial conditions and the constancy of rates. Both Christians and non-Christians must make assumptions about initial conditions and rates in order to make a scientific age estimate. However, since Christians and non-Christians have different worldviews, they often make different assumptions about rates and initial conditions.

Creationists, for example, believe that the universe was perfect and complete by the end of the very first week because the Bible gives us this information. On the other hand, secular scientists believe the universe started much differently and has gradually evolved to its present state. They generally assume the philosophy of naturalism — the belief that nature is "the whole show." God is not even a consideration, no matter how much evidence seems to point to Him. As such, a supernatural creation as described in Genesis is dismissed out-of-hand.

Creation scientists and secular scientists may also have different assumptions about the constancy of rates. Creation scientists are careful to include the effects of the worldwide flood in their estimation of ages; however, secular scientists dismiss the worldwide flood because they generally hold to the assumption of uniformitarianism — the belief that the present is the key to the past. Secular scientists assume that earth's geological features, such as mountains and canyons, have been produced by the same slow and gradual processes that we see operating today.

In the previous chapter, we saw how a rejection of biblical history has led the secular scientists to make vastly inflated estimates of the earth's age. By embracing the false philosophies of naturalism and uniformitarianism, the unbeliever is incapable of correctly interpreting the scientific evidence pertaining to the age of the earth. It is not a matter of intelligence, nor is it a matter of knowledge of the evidence. It is a matter of having the correct starting assumptions. Secular scientists start with the wrong assumptions and consequently obtain the wrong answer.

In this chapter, we will see that in most cases, *old-earth creationists also embrace the secular assumptions of naturalism and uniformitarianism.* It is curious that persons professing to believe the Bible would start with assumptions that are the opposite of what the Bible teaches. Most old-earth creationists seem to be unaware of this inconsistency. It is understandable that an unbeliever would reject the supernatural origin of the universe, or the fact that the world was judged by God and flooded with water. But it is disappointing that so many Christians have conformed their thinking to the ways of the secular world, perhaps without even realizing it.

Old-earth creationists are charged with using secular assumptions when doing science rather than presuppositions based on Scripture. False starting assumptions have caused them to err when interpreting data. A *sound,* logical argument must have conclusions that follow from the starting assumptions (the "premises"), *and the premises must be true.* Suppose I made the following argument:

All things with wheels are green	Major premise (F)
My car has wheels	Minor premise (T)
Therefore, my car is green	Conclusion (F)

This argument is logically valid — meaning the conclusion follows from the premises. However, the first premise is false — and so is the conclusion. Likewise, the estimates of the age of the earth made by old-earth creationists are unreliable. This is not because the logic is invalid, but because the starting assumptions are false — namely naturalism and uniformitarianism. Although, we will also see that there are some arguments in which the logic is faulty as well.

Old-Earth Arguments and Secular Assumptions

If the starting assumptions of a logical argument are wrong, then the conclusions will be unreliable. In the next sections, we will examine the *assumptions* behind some of the most common arguments for an old earth. We will start with radiometric dating of rocks. This section is a bit "meaty," but it is very important to understand because radiometric dating is so often cited as *proof* that the earth is billions of years old. We'll then move on to some other old-earth arguments and examine the assumptions behind them. In particular, we will look carefully at the assumptions of rates and initial conditions. We will find in all cases that old-earth arguments are based on the fallacious, anti-biblical assumptions of naturalism and uniformitarianism. Remember, if the assumptions of a dating method are wrong, then the conclusions cannot be trusted.

Radiometric Dating

One of the most commonly used arguments for an old earth involves the technique of radiometric dating. We are told that rocks "have been dated" to be billions of years old. Radiometric dating is supposed to tell how much time has elapsed since a rock was formed (from magma).

First of all, we *know* that radiometric dating is unreliable because it can be *tested* on rocks of known age. Indeed, geologists have taken rocks of which we know the age because they were formed from recent volcanic eruptions (the age of a rock is supposed to go back to the point of solidification). These rocks were then "age-dated" using the standard radiometric dating techniques. The results came back that these rocks were estimated to be hundreds of thousands to millions of years old,[1] when in fact their true age is only a few years. This is not an isolated incident; it is quite common. Dr Andrew Snelling, a geologist, points out several of these instances with potassium-argon (a common method for dating the earth at millions of years).[2] A few are listed below:

Potassium-Argon Dates in Error

Where?	When did the event occur?	Date by radiometric dating
Mt. Edna basalt, Sicily	122 B.C.	330,000–170,000 years old
Mt. Edna basalt, Sicily	A.D 1972	490,000–210,000 years old
Mount St. Helens, Washington	A.D. 1980	300,000–400,000 years old
Hualalai basalt, Hawaii	A.D. 1800–1801	1.76–1.44 million years old

1. John Morris, *The Young Earth* (Green Forest, AR: Master Books, 1998), 7th printing, p. 54–55
2. Andrew Snelling, " 'Excess Argon': The 'Achilles' Heel' of Potassium-Argon and Argon-Argon 'Dating' of Volcanic Rocks," Impact #307, Institute for Creation Research, found online here: http://www.icr.org/index.php?module=articles&action=view&ID=436. Accessed July 16, 2007.

Radiometric dating has been shown to *not work* on rocks of known age. Yet most secular scientists and other old-earth supporters *assume* that radiometric dating does work on rocks of unknown age. This is quite an obvious inconsistency.

Instead of asking whether or not radiometric dating is reliable, we should be asking, "*Why* is radiometric dating unreliable?" As we have already hinted, the answer lies in the assumptions that are involved in this method — assumptions about starting conditions and constancy of rates. As we saw in the previous chapter, these assumptions are strongly influenced by a person's worldview. It is our contention that the assumptions of *naturalism* and *uniformitarianism* are responsible for the incorrect age estimations. To support this claim, we need to examine how radiometric dating is supposed to work.

The methods used to obtain such estimates are based on measuring the relative amounts of radioactive substances (A) found in rocks. Radioactive elements have the ability to spontaneously change into other elements (B), releasing one or more forms of radiation in the process. Most elements in our everyday experience are not radioactive but stable. Nevertheless, rocks contain trace amounts of radioactive elements.

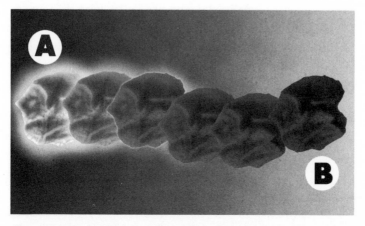

For example, a volcanic rock might contain traces of the radioactive element potassium-40. After some time, a fraction of that potassium-40 will have changed into argon gas. If we waited long enough, *all* the potassium-40 would have been converted into argon. We can measure the amount of potassium-40 and argon in rocks today. We also know the *rate* at which potassium-40 decays into argon; it is quite slow. It seems to follow that we could use this process to estimate the age of the rock in which these elements are found. So, if we measure the *current* amount of potassium-40 and argon in a rock, we could extrapolate backward (assuming the current decay rate) to find when the rock had only potassium-40 with no argon.

Hopefully, you were able to identify some of the assumptions involved in this technique. How do we know that the rock had no argon in it at the start? This is an assumption of the initial conditions. In this case, secular scientists claim to have good reasons to believe that there should be no argon in the rock when it first forms. Since argon is a gas, it can move through liquid fairly easily, but is somewhat trapped once the rock hardens. This certainly seems reasonable, but it is still an assumption and could be wrong in some instances. In fact, there are some cases where we actually *know* what the initial conditions were — because the rock is recent and its origin was observed. We know that in some cases today rocks form with argon already trapped inside. Yet it is often just *assumed* that more ancient rocks do not have this problem.[3]

Another assumption behind radiometric dating is that the *rate* at which the radioactive material decays has always been the same as it is today.[4] Once again, this stems from the assumption of uniformitarianism. The secular scientist reasons that if radioactive material decays slowly today, then it must *always* have decayed slowly. However, we should not arbitrarily assume that such rates have not changed with

---

3. The potassium-argon (K-Ar) method is a "model-age" technique, meaning that the initial conditions are assumed based on theoretical considerations alone. With some other radiometric dating methods (such as "isochron" methods), scientists attempt to estimate the initial amount of daughter elements using some clever procedures. However, in some cases two different methods will give two substantially different age estimates on the *same rock* — a clear indication that such the methods are unreliable regardless of how reasonable they might sound in principle. The details are beyond the scope of this book (they are discussed in the RATE books available on our website at answersingenesis. org), but the point remains that there is really no *scientific* way to know for certain what the initial conditions were unless the origin of the rock was directly observed.

4. Specifically, we mean that secular scientists assume that the "decay constant" for each radioisotope has not changed with time.

time. In fact, scientists have been able to speed up certain kinds of radioactive decay by as much as a billion times![5] We know that the rates can be accelerated today under the right conditions. Moreover, God could have accelerated radioactive decay in the past using supernatural means not available to us. Although God would not arbitrarily change such rates, we know that God has acted in a supernatural way in the past in order to accomplish His will. In particular, we know that God was acting in a supernatural way during the creation week. Therefore, we cannot necessarily assume that radioactive decay happened during the creation week at the same rate it happens today.

Additionally, God cursed the earth when Adam sinned (Gen. 3:17–18). The Bible provides only a few details of how the world was changed, such as thorns and thistles. Can we be certain that radioactive decay rates were not affected? The Christian would be hard-pressed to make such a claim on the basis of Scripture alone. Another important event in history that we must consider is the worldwide flood. Creation scientists have shown how the global flood could have caused many of earth's features to form much more quickly than they could at today's rates. Although it is difficult to believe that a flood could cause radioactive decay rates to change, the reverse is quite plausible. A drastic change in radioactive decay rates could have been the catalyst that God used to trigger the global flood. If radioactive decay rates were vastly accelerated, it would generate the heat necessary to initiate the plate tectonics associated with certain Flood models.

There are at least three times in history where the Bible-believing Christian has good reason to think that radioactive decay rates may not have been the same as they are today. In fact, a team of creation scientists from the *Institute for Creation Research* and the *Creation Research Society* have discovered very compelling evidence that radioactive decay rates have been drastically accelerated at one or more times in the past. They found that there is a tremendous amount of helium trapped in rocks. This helium is a by-product of radioactive decay, and since it is a very light (and "slippery") gas, it is able to slowly move through these rocks and escape. If the rocks were really millions of years old, the

---

5. http://www.answersingenesis.org/tj/v15/i2/acceleration.asp. Accessed July 16, 2007.

helium would have had plenty of time to escape. Since it obviously has not escaped, we can conclude that the rocks must be relatively young. The fact that a lot of helium has been produced indicates that a lot of radioactive decay has happened. Nevertheless, it must have happened quickly in the past few thousand years, otherwise the helium would have already leaked away. More details on this discovery are available in the book *Thousands . . . Not Billions* by Don DeYoung.[6]

It is clear that Christians have very compelling reasons to believe that radioactive decay rates have not remained constant throughout history. It certainly is understandable that a non-Christian would ignore the effects of creation, the fall of man, and the global flood. It is unfortunate that old-earth Christians would ignore these effects, choosing instead to blindly follow the secular philosophy of uniformitarianism.

It is important to realize that all radiometric dating techniques assume uniformitarianism. They assume that radioactive decay has happened at the same rate at which it occurs today. Yet we know that radioactive decay can be vastly accelerated under the right conditions, we know of at least three biblical events (creation, the Fall, and the Flood) where God may have altered radioactive decay to accomplish His will, and we have compelling scientific reasons to believe that decay rates have been accelerated in the past. Furthermore, we know that radiometric dating is unreliable when checked against the true age of rocks whose age is known. Therefore, from a logical perspective, radiometric dating of rocks cannot be considered reliable because it stems from faulty assumptions. People may strongly believe in the age estimates given, but this thinking is "blind faith," since the starting assumptions are wrong.

Annual Rings

Old-earth creationists will often point to so-called annual rings or layers in an effort to prove an old age for the earth. Dr. Ross has written:

> Tree rings, coral reefs, ice deposits in Antarctica and Greenland, and sedimentary layers in lakes and seas are like

---

6. Donald DeYoung, *Thousands . . . Not Billions* (Green Forest, AR: Master Books, 2005).

calendars in that they record the passing of years. Each year another ring or layer is added. By counting the rings or layers, an investigator can determine for how many years the tree, reef, ice deposit, or sediment has been in existence.[7]

These methods seem simple enough. Most people probably already know that you can estimate the age of a tree by counting its rings. But what assumptions have gone into the above computations? All of the above assume the constancy of rates. In other words, they have assumed that one tree ring is produced every year; however, this is not always the case. Scientists have observed that trees can form more than one ring per year, particularly in years in which mild weather produces a longer growing season. Interestingly enough, these are precisely the conditions that would have existed in many parts of the world during the Ice Age.

Creation scientists such as Mike Oard have found that an Ice Age lasting a few hundred years would have logically resulted when the global flood ended. Contrary to the mental picture many people have, many parts of the world would have had a very temperate climate with mild seasons (cool summers, relatively warm winters) during the Ice Age. This would have caused conditions favorable to the production of multiple tree rings in a single year. It is also quite obvious that in the colder regions, the weather during the Ice Age would have deposited many more layers of ice per year than normally happens today. Hence, the name "Ice Age"!

Many people don't realize how quickly ice layers can be deposited even today.[8] Near the top of an ice layer, there are consecutive bands of alternating oxygen isotopes. These bands form quasi-annually due to the alternating cycle of heat and cold (summer and winter). However, storms also produce a heat-cold cycle, but in a matter of days. The alternating layers become much less distinct farther down in the ice sheet. Those who believe in an old earth have already assumed that the ice layers are hundreds of thousands of years old, and therefore that

7. H. Ross, *A Matter of Days: Resolving a Creation Controversy* (Colorado Springs, CO: NavPress, 2004), p. 183.

8. http://www.answersingenesis.org/creation/v19/i3/squadron.asp. Accessed July 16, 2007.

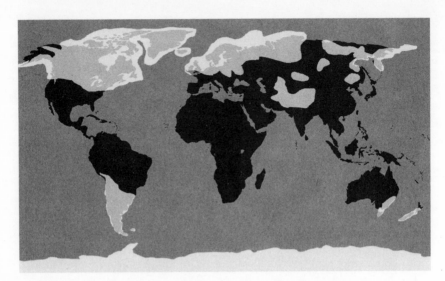

Ice sheet coverage during the Ice Age

such layers have been drastically compressed (vertically) and stretched (horizontally) near the base. As a result, they assume the indistinct annual layers thousands of feet down in an ice sheet would be perhaps 100 times more compressed than a creationist would assume.[9] Thus, a given volume of ice would be interpreted to have many times more annual layers in the uniformitarian view than in the creationist view. Old-earth assumptions have driven the old-earth conclusions. However, there is no scientific reason why such ice sheets cannot be laid down quickly. When we consider the effects of the post-Flood Ice Age, ice cores are consistent with the biblical time scale.[10]

One of the thickest coral reefs in the world is the Eniwetok Atoll in the Marshall Islands. Although coral reefs have been estimated to grow at rates of 0.8 to 80 millimeters per year at the surface, depth-sounding measurements have reported much higher growth rates. The reason for the difference is that low tides and intense sunlight can kill

9. See http://www.answersingenesis.org/tj/v15/i3/greenland.asp. Accessed July 16, 2007.

10. M. Oard, "Ice Cores vs the Flood" *TJ* 18(2):58–61, 2004; http://www.answersingenesis.org/tj/v18/i2/icecore.asp. Accessed July 16, 2007.

corals at the surface. In fact, some estimates for the growth rate at depth are as high as 414 millimeters per year. At this rate, the entire coral reef could form in less than 3,500 years.[11] Once again, we see that one of the thickest coral reefs in the world is consistent with the biblical time scale — even when we use rates measured today.[12] Clearly, coral reefs do not support an old earth.

Sedimentary layers can be laid down quickly in flood conditions, as we examined in the last chapter. Some layers contain alternating thick and thin layers of shale that are interpreted to form in summer and winter respectively.[13] Certain formations, such as the Green River Formation in Wyoming, contain millions of these layers, which are called "varves." Old-earth supporters have argued that varves prove the earth is very old. Once again, uni-formitarian assumptions play a key role. The old-earth creationists believe that in the past, varves have always been deposited annually — as they normally are today. However, similar alternating layers have been produced very quickly under the right conditions.[14] Moreover, well-preserved fossils of fish and birds are found in the Green River Formation. This indicates that conditions were much different than those that exist in lakes today, which do not normally provide the

> **Varve** — *a sediment consisting of two layers of material, one fine, the other coarse, which are interpreted to be deposited annually.*

11. "How Long Does a Coral Reef Take to Grow?" *Creation* 14(1):14–15, 1991; http://www.answersingenesis.org/creation/v14/i1/coral_reef.asp. Accessed July 16, 2007.

12. Bands within these corals are often interpreted as daily cycles; however, it is known that this is not always the case. Some corals have *more* than 365 bands within a "one-year" layer — others have *less*. Old-earthers have suggested that corals with more than 365 bands per year support the notion of millions of years, because earth allegedly rotated faster in the distant past (and thus had more than 365 days in one year). However, I've never heard an old-earther suggest that corals with *less* than 365 bands per year are from the future (when earth's rotation will supposedly be even slower than today). The inconsistency is clear.

13. See: http://www.answersingenesis.org/creation/v19/i3/greenriver.asp. Accessed July 16, 2007.

14. A. Snelling, "Sedimentation Experiments: Nature Finally Catches Up!" *TJ* 11(2):125–126, 1997; http://www.answersingenesis.org/tj/v11/i2/nature.asp, July 16, 2007.

conditions necessary for this kind of fossilization. Only by ignoring the effects of the global flood and other catastrophic events could we conclude that layers of rock, such as varves, represent vast ages.

Clearly, these old-earth arguments are all assuming uniformitarianism. Specifically, they ignore the effects of the global flood and the Ice Age that followed. When the effects of the Flood and the resulting Ice Age are included, we find that ice cores, lake sediments, coral reefs, and tree rings are consistent with the biblical time scale.

Ironically, each of these arguments against a young earth actually becomes evidence *for* a young earth when interpreted in light of Scripture! Take tree rings, for example. If we allow for the fact that trees can occasionally produce more than one ring per year, and if we count these rings, we find that the ages of the oldest trees in the world are only a few thousand years. This is consistent with the biblical time scale. The oldest-known living trees have roughly 4,600–4,800 rings.[15] It is therefore somewhat surprising, and perhaps a bit of a bluff, that an old-earth supporter would try to use tree rings to support the long-age position.

Distant Starlight

We also want to address some arguments that allegedly indicate an old *universe*. In our experience, the most commonly used argument for the supposed antiquity of the universe is "distant starlight." Some galaxies are so far away that presumably it should take billions of years for their light to reach earth. Since we do see these galaxies, obviously their light has arrived. Old-universe supporters claim this demonstrates that the universe is really billions of years old. We will now examine the assumptions that have gone into this estimation.

First, we must recognize that creationists and evolutionists agree on *some* of the assumptions involving distant starlight. We agree that the galaxies really are far away because the techniques that allow us to measure such distances are logically sound, repeatable methods; they are part of operational science. Furthermore, most creationists agree that the light from the stars was not created "already on its way." The

15. "Living Tree '8,000 Years Older than Christ' (?)" *Creation* 17(3):26–27, June 1995; http://www.answersingenesis.org/creation/v17/i3/living_tree.asp. Accessed July 16, 2007.

reason for this is that we see things happen in space; stars explode, pulsate, and so on. If we are merely observing light that was created in-transit, then none of these things have actually occurred. After all, the assumption that our senses are basically reliable (and therefore what we *see* is a reasonably accurate representation of reality) is a *biblical* assumption.

Also, the argument makes some assumptions concerning the constancy of rates. One such assumption is that the speed of light has not changed with time. If light were much faster in the past, then it could easily have traveled most of the distance from the galaxies to earth at its increased rate until it slowed down recently. Some creationists have suggested that this is the solution to the distant starlight argument; however, caution is in order. There are some good reasons to think that the speed of light really may be constant over time. The speed of light is "linked" to other constants in physics; if one changes, so do the others. It may be that the speed of light must have been pretty close to what it currently is in order for life to have been possible. Although such details are still being researched, most creationists believe that the constancy of the speed of light is probably a fairly good assumption. However, there are other rates that have been assumed to be constant in the distant starlight argument.

One other assumption is that the rate at which time itself flows is essentially constant. But Einstein showed that this is not the case. Under certain conditions, clocks will tick slower than in other conditions. This is called "time dilation" and it has been experimentally demonstrated. One creation-based cosmology uses this principle to get distant starlight to earth in only thousands of years. We have a number of resources discussing this exciting research,[16] and so we will not repeat the details here. The point to remember is that old-universe supporters have made a uniformitarian assumption concerning the constancy of time. They have assumed that the effects of time-dilation have never been significant as light travels through space. This critical assumption could be completely wrong; so, the conclusion that the universe must be old is unreliable.

---

16. D.R. Humphreys, *Starlight and Time: Solving the Puzzle of Distant Starlight in a Young Universe* (Green Forest, AR: Master Books, 1994).

The distant starlight argument also assumes naturalism since it supposes that the light arrived on earth entirely according to today's laws of nature. Is this reasonable? A Christian should not assume that this must be so. After all, stars began giving off light during the creation week when God was supernaturally creating the universe. Remember, the reason why the laws of nature are constant today is because God upholds the universe (Heb. 1:3) in a consistent way. The laws of nature describe the logical, consistent way that God has sustained the universe since He made it. But while God was creating the universe, He was acting in a way that is different than today. For example, He spoke stars and animals into existence. *The laws of nature are not adequate to describe how God created the universe.*

This is not to say that none of the laws of nature applied before God ended His work of creation. God was simultaneously sustaining the universe while continuing to create it. The description of the *sustaining* aspects of God's actions during the creation week might be what we would call the laws of nature. But God was also working in a *different* way than He works today. This cannot be overstated. When God created the lights in the firmament (the sun, the moon, and the stars) He made them to be for signs, seasons, days, and years, and "to give light upon the earth" (Gen. 1:14–15). Genesis 1:15 ends with the phrase "and it was so," suggesting that the stars fulfilled their purpose immediately, or at least on that day.

A consistent Christian must be open to the possibility that the mechanism God used to get the starlight to earth during the creation week cannot be understood in terms of today's "laws of nature." This thought may be disappointing to science-minded individuals because we want to know everything. And, of course, it is also possible that God did use "natural" means to get the starlight here. The point is that a Christian should not assume that this must be the case. Such an assumption is not warranted by the Bible.

There are other questionable assumptions that have gone into the distant starlight argument. For a more detailed discussion on these assumptions, see chapter 19 of *The New Answers Book.*[17] The purpose of this chapter is to show that old-earth (and old-universe) creationists have

17. Ken Ham et al., *The New Answers Book* (Green Forest, AR: Master Books, 2006).

used *unbiblical* assumptions to support their worldview. Once again, we have seen that the old-age proponents have fallaciously employed the secular assumptions of uniformitarianism and naturalism in order to arrive at their age estimate. Therefore, distant starlight cannot be considered to be a logical or reliable argument for an old universe.

Expansion of the Universe

Most biblical creationists believe that the universe is expanding, or has been expanded. Based on passages that describe God stretching out the heavens (Isa. 40:22; Job 9:8), we conclude that the universe is somewhat larger now than when it was first created. This expansion appears to be supported by scientific evidence as well, and most secular astronomers do believe the universe is expanding. The old-earth creationist Hugh Ross believes that this expansion is strong evidence for an "old" universe. His argument is unsound for more than one reason, and to be fair, I suspect that most old-earth supporters would not use it. I mention it here only because it is one of Hugh Ross's most common arguments[18] and because it is easy to see the faulty reasoning in it. Dr. Ross writes:

> So, careful measurement of the distances to galaxies, combined with their redshift values, can tell astronomers the rate of cosmic expansion. From that data they can then calculate how long the universe has been expanding.[19]

In other words, like secular scientists, Ross has assumed that the universe has always been expanding the way it is today.[20] Then he has extrapolated this expansion back in time while assuming that the universe started from (virtually) zero size. The assumption that today's rate of expansion has always applied[21] is the assumption of

---

18. In fact, it is the first argument Hugh Ross uses in his chapter on "Scientific Signs of Old-age" in his book *A Matter of Days*.
19. Ross, *A Matter of Days: Resolving a Creation Controversy*, p. 152.
20. Again, secular scientists do not assume a strictly constant rate of expansion. However, any changes in the expansion rate would be assumed to be due to the force of gravity and the "cosmological constant." No supernatural intervention is allowed in secular thinking.
21. Allowing for changes due to gravity and the cosmological constant only.

uniformitarianism. This is a particularly bad assumption in this case, because the Bible tells us that God himself stretches out, or has stretched out, the heavens. This may indicate that the bulk of this expansion was done supernaturally (using means that God does not normally use today).[22]

There is another assumption in this argument and it is quite strange. The old-universe argument assumes that the entire universe started with *no size*! This is an assumption of the *initial conditions*. The old-earth supporter would have us believe that all the mass and energy in the universe (and even space itself) were contained in a point with essentially no size called a "singularity." This idea certainly does not originate from Scripture.

The notion that this universe began as an infinitesimal point which suddenly catastrophically expanded forming matter, stars, galaxies, and everything else is called the "big bang." The big bang is what secular scientists believe created the universe. And many old-earthers have latched onto this secular model. In fact, Dr. Ross often refers to the big bang as the "creation event," presumably to make it sound biblical. Do not be fooled. The big bang is the *secular* model for the origin of the universe.

Why would anyone assume that the universe started with no size as a singularity? The answer is that secular scientists want to avoid a supernatural origin at all costs. Clearly, the creation of a large universe from nothing would require an act of God. Nothing large could ever pop into existence by itself; it would require a Creator, which is an unacceptable notion to the secular mind. However, at the very smallest level, particles seem to appear and disappear randomly. This is a very bizarre phenomenon in the field of quantum physics. Without going into details, it is sufficient to say that secular scientists hope to use what seems to be a "loophole" in physics. They hope that by pushing the problem to an infinitesimally small size it will allow them to believe in the creation of the universe from nothing without having to invoke a Divine Being. The problem for the secular scientist is that this doesn't

---

22. Of course, we can't be dogmatic on this point. But the consistent Christian must consider this possibility.

solve the problem, because even at very small sizes, particles do not truly come from nothing but from spacetime.[23]

The assumption that the universe began with no size is really an atheistic assumption and is a form of naturalism. Again, we want to stress that not all big-bang supporters are atheists. Many do believe in some sort of god, but they usually do not believe in the biblical God. The secular philosophy of naturalism dominates the thinking of scientists today. So the supernatural is excluded from the start. Many old-earth creationists have bought into the assumptions of the big bang without realizing its atheistic underpinnings.

We have seen that the expanding universe argument uses not just one, but *two* unbiblical assumptions. It assumes uniformitarianism (that the expansion rate has always been consistent with what we observe today) even though we have biblical reasons to think otherwise. It also assumes naturalistic initial conditions (that the universe began with no size). This particular old-universe argument is especially revealing. It confirms what we have stated previously, that old-earth creationists use the same assumptions as unbelievers when interpreting scientific data. This fact alone should cause believers to be very cautious about accepting old-earth claims.

Logical Fallacies

We want to briefly address some of the mistakes in logic that are occasionally committed by old-earth supporters. We do not mean to imply that these blunders are as common as the above arguments. For the most part, the conclusions of old-earth supporters follow logically from their incorrect assumptions; however, we have seen a substantial number of old-earth creationists and evolutionists employ the following logical fallacies.

First is the appeal to the majority. This is when a person argues that something must be true simply because a majority of people believe it. Of course, this is not a logical reason to believe something. A similar argument is the faulty appeal to authority. This is when

---

23. Anything that comes into existence requires a cause. This follows from the law of causality. Nothing can come from nothing. But spacetime is not "nothing"; it is something (because we can measure it!). And it seems to have the ability to produce and absorb short-lived particles called "virtual particles."

someone argues that a particular thing must be true because an expert in the field has said so. Although we certainly should respect people who are experts in their field, this does not mean that everything they say is true — even regarding matters in their own field of research. This is particularly clear when there are examples of other experts in the same field who disagree with each other.

Often the appeal to majority is combined with the faulty appeal to authority. "How could all those scientists be wrong about the age of the earth?" Although the question is meant to be rhetorical, it is easily answered. They start from the wrong assumptions due to a rejection of God's Word. Evolutionist[24] and old-earth supporter Eugenie Scott is fond of using this fallacy. Along with Glenn Branch, she wrote:

> The positive claims of young-earth creationism — that the universe and the earth were created ~10,000 years ago, that the Earth was inundated by Noah's Flood, and that all living things were created by God to reproduce "after their kind," thus setting limits on evolution — are unanimously rejected by the scientific community.[25]

This statement is obviously false, since there are many members of the scientific community who embrace the Bible's teachings. Although the majority of scientists reject a young universe, it can hardly be considered unanimous. And even if every single scientist believed in billions of years, it would not mean that it must be true. Remember, the majority of scientists also reject the resurrection of Christ. Just because a majority of scientists believe something does not make it true. This is not to say that we should ignore what scientists say. We should respect their knowledge. But we must always be careful to consider how their philosophy/worldview has colored their interpretation of the evidence.

Circular Reasoning

In a sense, virtually all old-earth arguments are circular. They assume the secular "old-earth" assumptions of uniformitarianism and

24. Like old-earth creationists, evolutionists generally accept the secular philosophies of naturalism and uniformitarianism.
25. E. Scott and G. Branch, "Evolution: What's Wrong with 'Teaching the Controversy,'" *TRENDS in Ecology and Evolution*, Vol. 18, Nov. 10, 2003, p. 501.

naturalism in order to "prove" that the earth is old. This circular logic may be due to the fact that many old-earth supporters are not aware of their own starting assumptions. However, astute thinkers should be able to identify the circular nature of many old-earth arguments. We pointed out earlier that radiometric dating is unreliable because it has been shown to give wrong age estimates on rocks whose ages are historically known. A prominent old-earth creationist has responded to this criticism. Note the circular reasoning in his statements:

> Supposed "evidence" against the reliability of radiometric dating focuses on the method's "flaws" or inaccuracies when applied outside its limitations. For example, uranium-238 radiometric dating, when applied to young samples, yields absurd dates. Why? With a half-life of 4.51 billion years, uranium-238 dating cannot be effective for measuring the age of any sample younger than a few hundred million years old.[26]

What's wrong with this reasoning? The problem is that *all* rock samples are "young." According to Scripture, they are all much younger than a few hundred million years. Therefore, uranium-238 dating will yield "absurd dates" for *all samples*. The old-earth creationist quoted above has assumed that radiometric dating really does give correct answers on rocks that are really millions of years old; but how do we know which rocks are really millions of years old? By uranium-dating them, of course. But this only works on "old" rocks. By the author's reasoning, we would have to *already know* the rock is ancient in order to use radiometric dating to prove that it is ancient. The reasoning is circular and thus proves nothing.

But the Universe *Looks* Old, Doesn't It?

We have heard a number of old-earth supporters make statements such as this: "If the universe really were young, then why does it look old?" We saw in the previous chapter that there are many evidences consistent with the biblical time scale. The statement that the universe "looks old" really reveals more about the person's starting assumptions than anything about the universe. Furthermore, this argument involves

---

26. Ross, *A Matter of Days: Resolving A Creation Controversy*, p. 178.

a number of fallacies: a failure to recognize the starting assumptions, the assumption of naturalism, and circular reasoning.

First, let's examine the starting assumptions behind this argument. If taken literally, the argument suggests that age can be identified by sight. This simply is not correct. How can the universe (or the earth or a rock) literally "look" old? Remember that age is not a substance that can be measured by instruments, and certainly not by eye. I could make a rock in a laboratory that is essentially identical to one found in nature. They would look identical, but would have vastly different ages. I could even place the same amounts of radioactive elements in the artificial rock, so it would give the same radiometric age estimate as the natural one. In order to know the age of something *for certain*, we would either need to have been present when the thing was created or have a historic record written by someone who was. When such information is missing, we can only make an educated guess about an object's age. Clearly, it is impossible to tell just by looking at the universe or the earth how old they are.

Of course, figuratively speaking, there is a sense in which something can "look" old or young, if we use the phrase loosely. For example, we might say that a person "looks" a particular age. But what do we really mean by this? Clearly, we don't mean that we can actually see someone's age as if it were a label stamped on his forehead. Rather, we mean that this person resembles other people, in some ways, whose age we do know. We might notice that Joe (whom we just met) is starting to lose his hair just like our good friend Greg (whose age we know either because he told us, or we grew up together, etc.) We might conclude that Joe is about the same age as Greg. Granted, people do not age at exactly the same rate, but it is not so far off that we would confuse teenagers with the elderly.

In order to make such age estimations, we need a large "sample size." We would have to observe many people whose age we know in order to make comparisons to a person whose age we are trying to estimate. Likewise, in order to correctly assess the age of the universe by sight alone, we would need to have a large sample of universes of different ages with which to compare it! But then, how would we know the ages of those other universes? Unless they are so very young that we had witnessed their creation, we would have to rely on eyewitness testimony of someone who had seen them created — perhaps God. Then we could say that our universe looks most like "Universe 103C" which God has told us is a particular age. However, as far as we know, God has only created the one universe. So, it just is not rational to say that the universe "looks" old when there is nothing with which to compare it.

In the same way, we cannot accurately say that the earth "looks" old, either. Although we do have a sample of other planets in the universe, we would have to know their ages in advance in order to compare with the earth. But how would we know their ages? By comparing them with still other planets, perhaps? We would have to know how old planets are in order to say how old they "look." Clearly such reasoning is circular. In fact, all the planets in the universe are the same age — except Earth! The Bible tells us that the stars were made on the fourth day of creation (Gen. 1:14–19). The Hebrew word for stars would also include what we call planets. All the celestial lights were made on the fourth day — three days after the creation of earth.

There is another fundamental flaw in arguing that the universe and earth "look" old. Many age-dating techniques overlook this simple point. It concerns the initial conditions — the way the universe and earth first started. To illustrate this point, we will go back to our analogy of estimating the ages of people. We can certainly get a very rough estimate of a person's age by their physical characteristics (size, hair color/amount, skin texture/wrinkles, etc.) since we have observed how people age. But suppose we could travel back to day 7, just one day after God created Adam. If we tried to estimate Adam's age in the same way we do with other people today, what would we conclude? You might say that Adam "looks" like a 30-year-old adult, but in fact, Adam was only one day old at this point.

Does this mean that God is dishonest? Was it deceptive of God to make Adam "look" 30 years old when his true age is only one day? Of course not. Remember, strictly speaking, something does not "look" old or young; age is an indication of history — not appearance. Why would we ever conclude that Adam "looks" older than he is? It is because we have made an incorrect assumption about initial conditions. We have assumed that Adam came into existence the same way people do today — conceived and born from previous people. This follows from the assumption of naturalism. When a baby is born, then it does take many years for him or her to become an adult.

In contrast, Adam did not need any time to become an adult. He looked exactly the way he was supposed to when God created him. If we incorrectly conclude that the one-day-old Adam "looks" 30 years old, this is an error on our part, not God's. Adam did not "look" 30 years old when he was created, although he may very well have looked similar (in some respects) to a typical 30-year-old man living today.

By incorrectly assuming that Adam came about by a natural process (the "ordinary" way God sustains the universe today), we would vastly overestimate his age, since Adam was supernaturally created. That is, God created Adam in a way He does not create people today: by forming him from the dust of the ground and breathing life into him. Remember that the earth and universe were also supernaturally created by God (Gen. 1:1). In contrast, the secular scientist believes that the earth and universe came about by the same natural processes in operation today. If we followed their lead, then we would likely conclude that the universe is much older than its true age, just as one might do with Adam. The assumption of naturalism leads to vastly inflated age estimates.

Some creationists have said that Adam was created with the "appearance of age." This is a subtle contradiction of terms because, as we've said, *age* cannot be *seen*. It would be better to say that Adam was created as a mature adult. In addition, the earth was created mature, and so was the universe. They were all fully operational from the moment God created them. Since secular scientists adhere to naturalism, they believe the earth and universe were created by the kinds of natural processes we see in operation today. This causes them to overestimate the age of things by a factor of millions.

Some Examples for Practice

In virtually all cases of old-earth arguments, there is an implicit unbiblical assumption of uniformitarianism or naturalism. To help you become better at recognizing these, we want to provide you with a couple of exercises. See if you can find the unbiblical assumption(s) in the following old-earth argument.

> Backward-revolving moons can also be explained in the context of great age. . . . The processes involved in moon capture, in radical tilting of a planet's rotation axis, and in significant slowing of a planet's rotation rate take millions of years to work their effects. They speak of age, not youth.[27]

Did you catch the unstated assumptions? The above argument assumes naturalism; it assumes that planets and moons formed by natural forces from a collapsing nebula. The possibility that God supernaturally created the planets and moons much as they appear now is not even considered. Yet the Bible makes it clear that the worlds were supernaturally created from nothing by God himself (Heb. 11:3). You might think that the above argument was offered by an atheist, but you would be mistaken. The author is an old-earth Christian. Like the atheist, he denies the possibility of a supernatural, *ex-nihilo* ("out of nothing") creation of the solar system by God. As we have said before, old-earth creationists use essentially the same assumptions as secular scientists.

Once you have learned the basic principles of identifying the starting assumptions in an age-estimate, it is easy to spot the flaws in old-earth arguments — even ones that are fairly technical. So let's try a more in-depth example from the field of astronomy. The old-universe argument is summarized in the next paragraph. Even without going into the physics details, it is possible to identify the secular starting assumptions.

The sun produces a tremendous amount of energy in its core by nuclear fusion. This energy is in the form of high energy *photons* — particles of light. These photons travel from the core to the surface of the sun. But they don't travel in a straight line because they are absorbed and re-emitted (in a random direction) by the hot solar plasma.[28] So it

---

27. Ibid., p. 205–206.
28. Plasma is high-temperature gas in which the electrons are stripped from the atomic nucleus.

takes quite a long time for the photons to "wander" randomly to the solar surface, where they escape to space. The process is called *photon diffusion*. Astronomy textbooks report that the photon diffusion time scale in the sun is about 100,000 years.[29] In other words, it would take an average of about 100,000 years for a photon created in the solar core to reach the surface of the sun. Since we do see photons (light) from the surface of the sun, the old-universe supporter argues that the sun must be *at least* 100,000 years old, and so the biblical time scale of about 6,000 years must be wrong.

Even though this argument is a bit more technical than most, it still suffers from the same flaws. The argument has employed secular assumptions to argue against the biblical time scale. In this case, the assumption is naturalism, which has led to incorrect initial conditions. In other words, it is assumed that we know that the photons on the surface of the sun today actually were produced in the core by the same natural processes in which they are produced today.

When God created the sun, it was shining right away — not because the photons had taken a long time to travel from the core, but because God made the sun hot! Notice that God did not need to create the photons directly (out of nothing). Simply by God giving the sun a high temperature, photons are produced from the plasma.[30] Today, that temperature is maintained by nuclear fusion in the core, but there is no rational reason to believe that the energy being released at the sun's surface today was once produced in the core. It was created supernaturally by God. So the secular assumption of naturalism is to blame for the inflated age-estimate.

There are many more such arguments that could be examined but have already been refuted in our other literature.[31] It is important to realize that all of them stem from the faulty and secular assumptions of naturalism, and uniformitarianism or in some cases, faulty logic. In fact, it is usually very easy to identify these assumptions in an old-earth argument. Go ahead and try it! Respectfully ask an old-earth

---

29. This is a rough approximation. Some estimates are much less, others, much more. However, they are essentially all greater than 6,000 years.
30. Hot plasma "glows." Photons are produced from the thermal energy.
31. Available at www.answersingenesis.org.

supporter why he or she thinks the earth is old. Pay attention to the starting assumptions. With some practice, you will quickly be able to identify the faulty reasoning of old-earth creationist (or evolutionist) arguments.

The Perpetual Motion Machine

A perpetual motion machine is a hypothetical device that can run forever without any input of energy. Many such machines have been proposed over the years. Some schematics appear on the surface very reasonable, but they always fail. Why? The laws of physics do not allow for such a mechanism. Specifically, the second law of thermodynamics insists that energy always goes from a useful to a useless form, and thus, any machine inevitably runs down unless it acquires new energy from an outside source. No matter how good a perpetual motion machine looks on paper, it could never work because it violates a law of physics. This law has demonstrated itself to be correct time and again.

Likewise, many arguments have been devised that supposedly prove the earth and universe are billions of years old. Some of these may seem good on paper, but they could never actually work because they violate the teaching of Scripture. The Bible has demonstrated itself to be correct time and again. We can have absolute confidence in what it says about the time scale of creation. Evolutionists and other old-earth supporters may continue to search for the proof that the universe is old, but their search is as futile as the search for a perpetual motion machine. No argument that goes against God's Word can possibly be sound.

Since the Bible undisputedly teaches a young earth, when someone claims that scientific evidence proves otherwise, we can be certain that they are mistaken. We have seen that faulty assumptions are responsible for inflated age estimates. Specifically, the unbiblical doctrines of naturalism and uniformitarianism cause unbelievers and other old-earth supporters to make incorrect assumptions about initial conditions and constancy of rates. Every "scientific" old-earth argument we have come across involves either incorrect starting assumptions or logical fallacies. In the spirit of 1 Peter 3:15, it is important to learn to identify these errors, so that we can give an answer to the unbeliever and to believers who are not yet strong in the faith. We should also remember the last phrase of 1 Peter 3:15; we must always answer with gentleness and respect.

Concluding Remarks

The Bible tells us that "all the treasures of wisdom and knowledge" are deposited in Christ (Col. 2:3; NAS).[32] Think about it: all truth is in Christ. God's Word is therefore the ultimate foundation for all knowledge. We must always strive to build our thinking on the rock of God's Word, not the shifting sands of man's opinion (Matt. 7:24–27).[33] Since it provides an infallible account of what God has done, the Bible is our supreme guide to interpreting the scientific evidence. It is because the Bible is true that science is possible! Since even unbelievers do accept that science is possible, it is clear that they know in their heart of hearts that the Bible is true. Sadly, they suppress that truth in unrighteousness (Rom. 1:18–20).

The secular world rejects the idea of a supernatural creation of the universe and earth. The unbeliever dismisses the catastrophic biblical flood of Genesis; the Bible says they "willfully forgot" that the world "perished, being flooded with water" (2 Pet. 3:5–6). Instead, the unbeliever embraces the philosophy of uniformitarianism — the idea that "all things continue as they were" (2 Pet. 3:4). The Bible tells us to beware of secular philosophies. "See to it that no one takes you captive through philosophy and empty deception according to the tradition of men, according to the elementary principles of the world, rather than according to Christ" (Col. 2:8).[34]

Many Christians have been taken in by the secular principles of naturalism and uniformitarianism. These false philosophies cause them to misinterpret scientific evidence and draw incorrect conclusions. Most people are not aware of the assumptions behind secular interpretations of data. They are inclined to accept the conclusions of the majority of scientists as truth without regarding the driving philosophies behind those conclusions. We are warned in 1 Timothy 6:20–21

---

32. Quotations from the NAS 1977.
33. Psalm 118:8.
34. Quotation from the NAS 1977.

to avoid "opposing arguments of what is falsely called 'knowledge.' "[35] We have seen how old-earth creationists have accepted the assumptions and conclusions of unbelievers, and how such secular thinking has led to severe "re-interpretation" of God's Holy Word.

We saw in the last chapter how Proverbs 26:4–5 suggest a "don't answer, answer" strategy for responding to a critic. We should never be fooled into accepting the critic's unbiblical assumptions ("don't answer" — verse 4), but we should show how such faulty assumptions would lead to an absurd or inconsistent conclusion if they were true ("answer" — verse 5). When we employed this strategy, we showed how the faulty assumptions of naturalism and uniformitarianism lead to inconsistent conclusions — age estimates that are much less than the billions of years required by secular origins models.

However, in this chapter we have seen that old-earth creationists have not followed this strategy. They use the "old-earth" assumptions of naturalism and uniformitarianism to "prove" that the earth is old. Such reasoning is circular and proves nothing. Rather than showing how the unbeliever's assumptions of naturalism and uniformitarianism lead to an inconsistent result, they have embraced these assumptions. By "answering the fool according to his folly" (Prov. 26:4) they have "become like him." Old-earth creationists have embraced the assumptions of unbelievers, and have become like them — refusing to believe the clear teachings of Scripture.

---

35. Ibid.

Chapter 9

The Verdict and Recommendations

The Lord holds Christians to a high standard, and so does the world. The use of uninformed and misleading arguments does not bring honor and glory to the name of Christ. Only when fellow believers are treated with respect and dignity will progress be made in this important debate.

Most importantly, God will be glorified when His followers seek to honor His Word from the very first verse to the very last verse. Christians have no need to compromise the Word of God with the opinions of man. When science can help clarify gray areas of Scripture, then it should be used cautiously; this is called the "ministerial role of science." However, science should never be set up as equal to or above Scripture; that is, science should never be used in a "*magisterial* role." As we saw in chapter 7, science requires the principles of Scripture in order to exist. Therefore, science cannot be more authoritative than the Bible on which it stands. In addition, Christians can trust the Word of the One who was there "in the beginning" and chose to reveal His works to His people. It is sad that so many believers place more trust in the opinions of fallible men than in their omniscient and holy God. Charles Spurgeon spoke so eloquently about the danger of compromise when he stated:

Neither may we hope to gain by being neutral, or granting an occasional truce. We are not to cease from conflict, and try to be as agreeable as we can with our Lord's foes, frequenting their assemblies, and tasting their dainties. No such orders are written here. You are to grasp your weapon, and go forth to fight.[1]

Old-earthers are charged with compromise in the area of the age of the earth and the extent of the Flood. Their ideas do not originate in Scripture but come from their philosophical beliefs. They have accepted the majority view among scientists and have attempted to make the Bible fit this view. Yet the Bible cannot incorporate these views without contradicting itself. As such, these views cannot be correct.

Old-earth creationists are hereby found guilty of compromise concerning the age of the earth and the extent of the Flood. Fortunately for Christians, God has already paid the penalty for sins and believers are already forgiven. However, old-earthers are sternly warned to stop trying to accommodate the false philosophies of the day and learn to fully trust in the Word of the omniscient God.

Recommendations for Improving the Debate

Debate can be healthy for the Church. Because of man's fallibility, it is guaranteed that differences of opinion will arise. It is in these moments that the Church must show the world how to behave properly. Unfortunately, believers often allow their emotions, biases, and pride to get the best of them. There are three major areas that must be worked on from both sides of this debate. Only then can "iron sharpen iron" (Prov. 27:17).

First, both sides need to practice academic integrity. This would entail applying rigorous discipline to scientific endeavors. Rather than making spectacular claims based on sketchy evidence or searching for the "magic bullet" that "proves" a particular age of the earth, Christians need to continue to develop scientific models that fit the evidence. The past decade has witnessed a great deal of progress for young-earthers, but there is still work to be done. For example, Dr. Russell Humphreys'

---

1. Spoken by Charles Spurgeon in a sermon entitled "The Sword of the Spirit" delivered on April 19, 1891, at the Metropolitan Tabernacle.

white hole cosmology uses the scientific data available today to construct a viable framework that is consistent with the evidence. Dr. John Baumgardner has used computer modeling to demonstrate rapid plate tectonic movement as a result of the Flood. Further scientific research in these fields and others can only help the young-earth creationist movement.

For the old-earther, this recommendation will be a tougher pill to swallow. The many weak and misleading arguments refuted in this book must be abandoned. Old-earthers must learn to base their theories on the words of Scripture rather than on fallible men whose theories are constantly changing. Old-earth creationists must also stop using arguments that have already been answered by mainstream young-earth organizations. Finally, academic integrity demands that old-earthers stop attacking the arguments made by those on the fringe of young-earth creationism and treating them as if they are the mainstream arguments. They need to deal directly with the arguments from the leading young-earth organizations, such as *The Institute for Creation Research*, *Answers in Genesis*, and *The Creation Research Society*.

Second, personal attacks are unnecessary and unbiblical. In 2 Corinthians 10:5, Paul instructed his readers that we are in the business of "casting down arguments" not people. Perhaps the most frustrating part of any debate occurs when one or both sides resort to *ad hominem* attacks to advance their particular agenda. Arguments should be evaluated on their merit, and not on the person making the claim.

In the same way, old-earthers must refrain from labeling young-earth creationists as unscientific and on a level of those who hold to geocentricity and a flat earth. While demonstrating Martin Luther's belief in the scientific accuracy of Scripture, Dr. Geisler sought to lump Luther's views on geocentricity in with his belief that the days of Genesis were 24 hours long.[2] Logic once again escapes Geisler. Luther's belief in geocentricity had nothing to do with his belief in a young earth. Even though he believed Scripture taught both of these ideas, the falsity of one does not disprove the other. They are completely unrelated.

These types of accusations do nothing to encourage honest discussion of the views. They are designed merely to warrant an emotional

---

2. Norman L. Geisler, *Systematic Theology, Volume I* (Minneapolis, MN: Bethany House, 2002), p. 300–301.

response from the other side. Christians, both old-earth and young-earth, should be above this type of argumentation.

Finally, old-earthers must endeavor to develop a coherent theological position that is consistently supported by Scripture. We contend that it is not possible to do this within an old-earth framework. However, old-earth creationists are welcome to attempt to refute our position using legitimate hermeneutics, sound logic, and appropriate ministerial use of science. Rather than basing their view on questionable or unlikely interpretations of the text, they must show that the Bible provides strong support for their view. Just because a certain Hebrew or Greek word *can* be translated in a particular way does not mean that it *should* be interpreted that way. The interpretation depends on context. If old-earthers are forced to adopt a questionable interpretation on several, if not all, of their points, then this does not strengthen their position. In fact, with the addition of each questionable interpretation, their position weakens.

Old-earth creationists must be able to conclusively demonstrate that Scripture repeatedly not only allows for, but also implies, an age of the earth in excess of 10,000 years. Non-specific comments about the antiquity of the universe simply do not accomplish this. For example, 2 Peter 3:5 reveals that "the heavens were of old." From Peter's perspective, 4,000 years would have been a long time, especially when one considers that the Jewish people of the day did not hold to a notion of billions of years. What the old-earth creationist has to be able to show is that the Bible speaks clearly for his or her position and at the same time conclusively against the young-earth view. This has never been accomplished.

An important principle of biblical hermeneutics is that Scripture cannot contradict Scripture. Any view that forces the Bible to contradict itself cannot be accurate. This is precisely what old-earth creationism does on numerous occasions. Based on this overview of the theological arguments used by the old-earthers, it is clear that young-earth creationism is the only viable biblical position. It has the support of the New Testament writers and the majority of leaders throughout Church history. It even has the backing of our Lord Jesus Christ. It is time for pastors, professors, and laypeople to stop being intimidated by arguments for an old earth. God's Word clearly teaches a young earth and that settles the matter.

Final Thoughts

You have nearly reached the end of this book. If you began this book as a young-earth creationist, we trust that your confidence in this view has been greatly strengthened. If you started out as someone who was unsure which position was correct, we believe that what you have read is more than enough information to demonstrate the fact that old-earth creationism simply cannot stand up to biblical and scientific scrutiny. As such, it must be rejected. If you began as an old-earth creationist and were not swayed in your conviction, then we hope and trust you have seen the weaknesses of many of the arguments used by old-earthers. We hope that you have read enough to convince you that the young-earth position is the only viable, biblical stance one can take. However, if you have not changed your mind, we encourage you to help improve this debate by utilizing sound arguments in a loving manner.

Perhaps you have been convinced that the Bible obviously teaches a young earth but struggle with reconciling that with modern scientific opinion. Be encouraged! The billions of years and evolutionary theories are simply houses of cards. We have shown the fallacies of such arguments in chapter 8. Old-earth science is based on naturalism; but if naturalism were true, science would be impossible. God's Word is truth and true science will always line up with it. God created the universe, and He knows how it works! Have confidence in the author of Scripture and take some time to read through some of the books listed in Appendix F. These will go a long way in strengthening your faith and providing answers to some of the tough questions.

When dealing with the question of the age of the earth, the best place to find answers would be from a history book. In the Book of Genesis, the Bible provides a record of the very beginning of time and space. This record is inspired by the God who was there and who made all things. His record shows that He made everything during a span of six days of approximately 24 hours each and that this occurred about 6,000 years ago. Since God cannot lie, then this record must be true.

It does not matter how many fallible men disagree with it. Jesus boldly proclaimed, "Heaven and earth will pass away, but My word will by no means pass away" (Matt. 24:35).

Let's Get Practical

We have discussed this issue with numerous pastors and other Christian leaders. Often we have been told that it just is not that important because it is not practical or is merely a side issue. Before jumping to this conclusion, please consider the following real-life testimony of one of the authors (Tim).

In the summer of 2006, I was diagnosed with Acute Promyelocitic Leukemia (APL or M3 for short). My doctor told me that when I checked into the hospital I was "on the razor blade of life. Too much or too little of anything" and I would die. In fact, for a few consecutive mornings, he left me with the following charge: "Tim, your job for today is to stay alive and wake up in the morning." In other words, I was in very critical condition.

Fortunately, my type of leukemia was the most treatable kind and I have been in remission since September of 2006. I spent a month in the hospital during what is known as the induction stage of my treatment. Throughout that time, I suffered from the debilitating effects of the disease and through many of the side effects associated with chemotherapy. All told, I went through four rounds of chemotherapy and several months recovering from the symptoms of the disease and the treatment.

The reason that I share this with you is not for you to feel sorry for me. I want to show you how important this issue really is. Please think about the following point for a few minutes so that it sinks in.

Leukemia is a type of cancer that affects the blood. Scientists have found evidence of cancer in fossilized bones that are allegedly much older than the time of Adam and Eve. Yet after Adam and Eve were created, God looked at everything He had made and declared that it was "very good" (Gen. 1:31). This means that our loving Creator must think that cancer is "very good."

This point cannot be overstated. Cancer has affected the lives of so many people. It nearly took my life and has harmed or killed millions of people and animals around the world. Yet, if the old-earth view is correct, then cancer must be "very good." Think about how this attacks the goodness and holiness of God! We know that cancer is not "very good." In His earthly ministry, Jesus healed the sick; why would He do this if sickness were "very good"? Biblically, we can be confident that cancer is not something that God would call "very good." I can tell you from personal experience that it is an awful disease.

During my time in the hospital, I often thought about what my mindset would be if I were an old-earth creationist. After all, if cancer had been part of God's "very good" creation, then my God must really like the disease that was taking away my life. Is it even possible to view Him as a God of love if one is an old-earth creationist? We realize that old-earth creationists do believe that God is a loving God; however, the logical conclusion of their view is that He is a God who enjoys death and suffering. Fortunately, most old-earth creationists do not carry out their viewpoint to its logical conclusion. Many unbelievers have made this connection and have rejected the Gospel message because they cannot believe in a God of love since this world is full of death and destruction. In fact, this is the very point that pushed Darwin over the brink of unbelief when his precious daughter Annie died at age ten.

Since my diagnosis, I have heard many fellow believers say, "We don't know why God allows these things to happen." In fact, a pastor who refuses to take a stand on the old-earth/young-earth debate said these very words to me. As I thought about his words, I realized that he really does not know why God allows these things to happen. In fact, countless Christians have struggled to find an answer to this question and oftentimes their pastors or teachers do not provide adequate responses. But I know the answer. I know exactly why I had leukemia and nearly died. Are you ready for this? It is because I am a sinner. The Bible says that "the wages of sin is death" (Rom. 6:23). As a result, I deserve to die! It was not that I committed a particular sin that resulted in leukemia, but because I am a sinner living in a sin-cursed world it is always possible for something bad to happen to me.

Having this perspective on things put my mind at ease during this entire ordeal. I can honestly tell you that I never asked "Why me?" I knew the reason. The questions I had were "Why did it take so long?" and "Why not everyone else?"

If his view is correct, the old-earth creationist would be completely justified in asking God "Why me?" He could go one step further and ask why God would create a planet so full of death and suffering. The old-earth position simply is not consistent with a loving God. This is why this issue is extremely practical. If somebody accepts unbiblical teaching, such as old-earth creationism, then he accepts an unbiblical view of God. Nothing could be more practical than making sure that our view of God is correct.

On the other hand, only the young-earth creationist can make sense of the situation. God created a perfect world with no death, no disease, no bloodshed, and no suffering. He created Adam and Eve and told them they could serve Him or disobey Him. He even told them what the consequences of disobedience would be (Gen. 2:17). They chose to disobey Him when they ate of the fruit of the tree of knowledge of good and evil. As a result of their disobedience, God cursed His creation and now we are suffering from the consequences of the sin of our first parents.

It is not God's fault that so many terrible things happen in this world. It is our fault. We cannot blame God. We can only blame ourselves for the mess we are in and look forward to the day that God will make all things new.

It is time for the Church to stop compromising with an unbiblical theology that views God as a God of death, disease, and suffering. It is time to stop compromising the clear words of God's inspired Word and start trusting fully in what He said He did.

Appendix A

Other "Interpretations" of Genesis

T he purpose of this section is to define some of the interpretive schemes that have arisen since the idea of vast ages became popular in the late 18th and early 19th centuries. Please bear in mind that old-earth theologies were essentially non-existent prior to 1800. This fact alone provides strong evidence that these views are not derived from the Bible. Instead, they are an attempt to accommodate the long ages promoted by uniformitarian science.

The Gap Theory

This was the first attempt to harmonize the biblical account of creation with the idea of vast ages. It claims that a huge time gap (perhaps several billion years) exists between Genesis 1:1 and Genesis 1:2. In the most popular "ruin-and-reconstruction" version, it is said that during this time Satan rebelled and led creation in rebellion against God. As a result, God destroyed this original creation with the flood of Lucifer. Gap theorists believe that Genesis 1:2 describes the conditions of the world following this flood.

A young Presbyterian minister, Thomas Chalmers, began to preach this idea in 1804. In 1814, he published this idea and the gap theory began to enjoy a great deal of acceptance in the Church. Gap theorists often argue that the word translated as "was" in most English versions of Genesis 1:2 should actually be translated "became" as in "the Earth *became* formless and void." However, this is unwarranted by context. The gap theory suffers from a number of hermeneutical problems.

First, time cannot be inserted between Genesis 1:1 and Genesis 1:2 because verse 2 does not follow verse 1 in time. Verse 2 uses a Hebrew grammatical device called a "waw-disjunctive." This is where a sentence begins with the Hebrew word for "and" ("waw" וֹ) followed by a noun such as the "earth" ("erets" אֶרֶץ). A waw-disjunctive indicates that the sentence is describing the previous one — it does not follow in time. In other words, verse 2 is describing the conditions of the earth when it was first created. Hebrew grammar does not allow for the insertion of vast periods of time between Genesis 1:1 and 1:2.

Second, Exodus 20:11 clearly teaches that everything was created in the span of six days — this is the basis for our work week. This passage clearly precludes any possibility of vast periods of time between any of the days of creation.

Third, most versions of the gap theory put death and suffering long before Adam's sin. So the gap theory suffers from many of the same doctrinal problems as the day-age view. For a full refutation of the gap theory, please read *Unformed and Unfilled* by Weston W. Fields.[1]

Theistic Evolution

This view claims that God used evolution as a means of bringing about His creation. Conservative Christians typically reject this idea because it attacks the idea that Adam was made in the image of God and from the dust of the earth. Instead, he and Eve simply evolved from apelike creatures. Many liberal scholars accept this view and see no problem with incorporating evolutionary principles into the Bible.

Theistic evolution impugns the character of God by blaming Him for millions of years of death, bloodshed, disease, and suffering. A world with these things in it could hardly be called "very good." As with day-age and gap theories, theistic evolution is not supported by Scripture, and has numerous doctrinal problems.

---

1. Weston Fields, *Unformed and Unfilled* (Green Forest, AR: Master Books, 2005).

The Day-Age Theory

This view is appropriately named. Its proponents claim that each of the days of creation was an extremely long period of time. In support of this view, they usually quote Psalm 90:4 and 2 Peter 3:8, which state "one day is as a thousand years."

The problem with citing these verses is that they are not even referring to creation. The passage in 2 Peter, for example, is referring to the Second Coming. These verses are simply teaching that God is not limited by time. He is beyond the confines of His creation, not bound by it.

The day-age theory became popular after George Stanley Faber, a respected Anglican bishop, began to teach it in 1823. For the past two centuries, this view has been tweaked to accommodate changing scientific beliefs. Some day-age proponents believe in theistic evolution; others believe in "progressive creation" as described below. The day-age view is based on a hermeneutical error called an "unwarranted expansion of an expanded semantic field." In other words, it is assumed that because the Hebrew word for "day" can mean "time" (in a general sense) in some contexts, then it is permissible to interpret it to mean "time" in Genesis 1. However, as we've shown in this book, the context of Genesis 1 does not allow for such a possibility.

Progressive Creation

This version of old-earth creationism is probably the most popular of the compromise views in the Church today. Most progressive creationists are also day-age supporters; they believe that each of the creation days was a long period of time. However, rather than accepting biological evolution, progressive creationists believe that God created in stages over many millions of years. They believe that God created certain animals millions of years ago and then they died out. Then God created more animals that died out. Eventually, He got around to making humans.

Although many progressive creationists reject biological evolution, they generally accept astronomical and geological evolution. Like theistic evolutionists, progressive creationists believe in millions of years of death, disease, suffering, and bloodshed before Adam's sin. Such positions inevitably undermine the Gospel message.

Dr. Hugh Ross' organization, Reasons to Believe, is the leading promoter of this view today. Dr. Jonathan Sarfati wrote a comprehensive critique of this view entitled *Refuting Compromise* (Master Books, 2004). This book is a rather exhaustive critique of the theological and scientific claims made by Dr. Ross in his various books and lectures.

Framework Hypothesis

This view is rather hard to understand. The late Meredith Kline from Westminster Theological Seminary was the view's major spokesperson. Andrew S. Kulikovsky did a good job of explaining it in the *Creation Technical Journal* (Vol. 16, Issue 1, p. 40). He wrote:

[The framework hypothesis] takes the Genesis account of Creation as a theological framework rather than a strictly historical, chronological account. It is important to note that proponents of the framework view do not deny that the people and events alluded to in the Creation account are essentially historical. It should be obvious, however, that in denying the historical and chronological nature of the account, they have very little basis for this acceptance.

The reason this view is so confusing is due to the amount of doublespeak utilized by its supporters. Oftentimes, Genesis 1–11 is described as being a "myth." When asked if this means that it is not true, they respond with an emphatic, "No! It's a myth!" As you can see, this can be rather confusing to anyone with a basic understanding of logic and the English language. The term "myth" usually implies that something is fictional or made up. Nevertheless, the framework hypothesis suffers from many of the same fatal problems inherent in each of the other views. See Appendix B for more information.

Other Views

There have been other attempts to synchronize the Bible's account of creation with the evolutionary viewpoint. Two of these views have diminished in popularity in the past few decades. The *revelatory day* view states that God gave Moses a series of visions of His creative work. These visions lasted for six days. The obvious problem with this view is that there is absolutely no scriptural support for it. The Bible never even hints that this may have been the case, so it is based on a lack of evidence. The other view is called the *literal-day-with-gaps*. This view states that each of the days of creation was a literal day, but there were huge gaps of time in between each day. This view suffers from many of the same problems as the day-age theory and the gap theory.

Numerous other minor views have been proposed in an effort to harmonize Genesis 1–11 with secular scientific opinion. Those described here represent the vast majority of believers who seek this harmonization. The very fact that so many views exist provides evidence that each of them is inherently flawed.

Problems with Other "Interpretations"

Problem/Theory	Gap Theory	Theistic Evolution	Day-Age Theory	Progressive Creation	Framework Hypothesis
Places death before sin	X	X	X	X	X
Sun created before earth	X	X	X	X	X
Satan fell before end of creation week	X	X	X	X	X
Dinosaurs did not live with man	X	X	X	X	X
Noah's flood was not a worldwide catastrophe	X	X	X	X	X
All creation was not "very good"	X	X	X	X	X
Symbiotic relationships non-existent	X	X	X	X	X
Other "order of events" conflicts	X	X	X	X	X

There are certainly many more problems that each of these views create. These consist of biblical and scientific problems. These selected examples should be more than enough to make the point.

Death before Sin

This is perhaps the biggest problem created by each of the compromising views. The Bible makes it very clear that there was absolutely no death before Adam sinned. Romans 5:12 states, "Therefore, just as through one man sin entered the world, and death through sin. . . ." First Corinthians 15:21 states, "For since by man [Adam] came death, by Man [Jesus] also came the resurrection of the dead." These passages are dealing primarily with human death, but it is also clear from Romans 8 that sin affected all of creation. Scripture is clear that animal death was instituted when Adam sinned, as we will show below.

Each of the old-earth views places death, bloodshed, disease, and suffering before Adam's sin. However, the Bible teaches that all was "very good" (Gen. 1:31) when God made it. Would God have called everything that He had made "very good" if it were full of death and suffering? Absolutely not! Remember, Jesus healed the sick and resurrected the dead. Why would He do these things if these people were already in a "very good" state? Death and suffering were not a part of the original creation but only entered because of the fall of man. Further evidence for this is provided by the fact that people and animals were originally allowed to eat plants only (Gen. 1:29–30).

Besides the fact that it contradicts the Bible, the reason that this problem is so severe is because it undermines the very meaning of the atonement. When Adam sinned, the Bible states that God made coats of skins for Adam and Eve. Here is the first indication of death in the Bible. God killed an animal (quite possibly a lamb or lambs — although the Bible does not say directly) to make these coats. This would have served as a graphic portrayal of the consequences of Adam's sin. Adam would have seen blood being shed for the first time in atonement for sin. What a powerful picture of the devastating effects of sin and of the coming Messiah. However, if the world were already full of death and bloodshed (as old-earthers teach) then this action would be meaningless. Adam would certainly not infer that the wages of sin is death. If death and suffering were already in the world, then sin did virtually nothing. If the foundations for the gospel are undermined, then why did Jesus Christ come to earth to die on the cross for our sins? He was the ultimate sacrifice, the Lamb of God who takes away the sins of the world. But if there was death before sin, what did sin do? If it was part of the original creation, then why did Jesus need to shed His blood?

The old-earth views still have many additional problems in this area. As a result of Adam's sin, God cursed the ground (Gen. 3:17–18) to bring forth thorns and thistles. Yet we find thorns and thistles in the fossil record that are allegedly millions of years old, according to old-earthers. Why would God curse the ground with thorns if they were already in abundance on the earth? It just does not make sense and it does not line up with God's Word.

The Sun Created before the Earth

Because each of the old-earth views accepts the evolutionary time scale of "billions of years" for the age of the earth and universe, they run into another glaring problem. Secular origin models of the solar system (which each of these theories embrace) state that the sun was formed *before* the earth. However, according to the Bible, the earth was made on day 1 while the sun was created on day 4.

In an attempt to circumvent this problem, Dr. Ross claims that the Bible teaches that the sun "appeared" or became visible on the earth

Big Bang	Stars	Sun	Molten Earth	First Oceans
15 Billion years ago	10 Billion years ago	5 Billion years ago	4.5 Billion years ago	3.8 Billion years ago

Water covered Earth	Dry land and plants	Sun, moon, and stars	Sea and flying creatures	Land animals and man
Day 1-2	Day 3	Day 4	Day 5	Day 6

on day 4. He believes that the sun existed long before the earth. However, the Hebrew language does not allow for this. The Hebrew word used in the creation of the sun (the "greater light") is *asah*, which means "to make." It is very different than the Hebrew word *ra'ah*, which is translated "appear" (as the land does in Genesis 1:9). So, this is another example of twisting Scripture to fit preconceived notions. It is absolutely essential to allow the Bible to speak for itself rather than trying to fit one's ideas into the Bible. God does not need the help of modern secular scientific opinion.

The people that hold to these compromise views will often ask where the light came from on the first three days. The simple answer is that the Bible does not tell us but it does state that there was light. The sun is not necessary for day and night — only a directional light source is needed. The Bible is clear that light was in existence since the first day: And God said, "Let there be light." Revelation 21:22–22:5 may provide the answer to this question. It states that in the New Jerusalem there will be no need of the sun because God's glory will illuminate it. This is a possibility as to where the light came from for the days in question. Another possibility is that God may have used a temporary light source. However, since the Bible does not tell us, we should be cautious and not dogmatic with our speculations.

Satan Fell before the End of the Creation Week

Once again, the compromise views create a theological dilemma. The gap theory (the ruin-and-reconstruction version) teaches that Satan fell and led earth in a rebellion against God prior to Genesis 1:2. The other theories teach death and suffering prior to the fall of man. They also claim that Satan rebelled prior to the end of the creation week. This concept is problematic for the following reasons.

a) God stated that everything He had created was "very good" at the end of the sixth day. We know that Satan was created at some point during the creation week, because Exodus 20:11 states that God made everything in the earth, the sea, and the heavens in six days. Satan is included in this. Job 38:7 teaches that the angels rejoiced when God laid the foundations of the earth. This indicates that the angels were made early on in the creation week. They would not have fallen before the sixth day because everything God made was still "very good."

b) Ezekiel 28:12–19 suggests that Satan was in Eden and was perfect "till iniquity was found in" him. How could Satan have been in the Garden of Eden and be perfect if he fell long before the Garden was ever created?

Man Did Not Live with Dinosaurs

It is commonly taught that dinosaurs and man did not live together. Evolutionists claim that dinosaurs died out some 65 million years ago. Each of these compromising views also teaches this. However, it can easily be demonstrated that this is not the case.

The Bible teaches that land animals (everything that creeps upon the earth) were made on the sixth day of creation — the same day human beings were created. Dinosaurs were land animals. Therefore, human beings and dinosaurs most certainly lived at the same time, since they were created on the same day. This is a logical deduction, even if the Bible didn't mention dinosaurs specifically. However, the Bible does indeed describe animals that resemble dinosaurs and other extinct reptiles such as plesiosaurs or flying reptiles. (The latter are not classified as dinosaurs, but are equally devastating to old-earth views.) In the Book of Job, God tells Job about the behemoth and the leviathan. Many study Bibles will include a text note that these were probably the elephant or hippopotamus and the crocodile. It is important to remember that the text of Scripture is inspired, but the text notes are not. These editors were obviously influenced by the evolutionary idea that dinosaurs died out long before man arrived on the screen.

A brief examination of this passage will demonstrate that the text notes in these Bibles are wrong. The description of this creature in Job 40 perfectly fits that of a sauropod dinosaur such as *Brachiosaurus*. Would the elephant's tail or hippo's tail remind anyone of a "cedar tree" (v. 17)? While it may be true that the word translated as "tail" could possibly be rendered "trunk," there is another problem. If the word should be "trunk," then why does Job 40:24 state that this creature has a nose? This statement rules out the possibility of behemoth being an elephant. The leviathan is described as being capable of breathing fire and raising itself up. When was the last time you saw a crocodile breathe fire or rise up?

In January of 2004, Dr. Mary Schweitzer discovered soft tissue from a *Tyrannosaurus Rex* leg bone. Although she believes the fossil is millions of years old, evolutionists are at a loss as to how the soft tissue could have been preserved for so long.[1] This is perfectly consistent with the biblical teaching that dinosaurs were created on the same day as man.

Literally hundreds of cultures from around the world have dragon legends. The description of these creatures often matches that of dinosaurs. Dinosaur pictographs have been found all over the world. How could ancient people have known about these creatures, since they did not have the fossil remains? Also, numerous historical records exist that tell of men fighting against dragons. Are all of these simply fairy tales or is it possible that some of them are historical events? The fact that these occur in numerous cultures around the globe is a strong argument in favor of men and dinosaurs existing together.

Also, the very idea that God created billions upon billions of animals for millions of years before man ever came on the scene strikes against the very purpose of the creation. In Genesis 1:28, God gave man dominion over all of the earth and its creatures. What possible reason would God have in making creatures such as dinosaurs, and then allowing them to suffer

1. See *Discover* magazine's article at http://www.discover.com/issues/apr-06/features/dinosaur-dna/. Accessed July 18, 2007.

and die millions of years before man ever had a chance to enjoy and appreciate these marvelous creatures? The answer, of course, is that He did not do it this way. God created all the original kinds of animals and Adam and Eve within a two-day time period — days 5 and 6 of the creation week.

Noah's Flood Was Not a Worldwide Catastrophe

In terms of geology, either the bulk of the fossils were deposited in a global flood or they were deposited over millions of years. It would be geologically absurd to suppose that there was a worldwide flood that deposited no new fossils, nor disturbed any previous ones. Therefore, old-earth creationists must deny a worldwide flood. But, the Bible makes it clear that Noah's flood was global — the waters covered all the high hills under the whole heaven (Gen. 7:19) This was examined in detail in chapters 5 and 6.

All of Creation Was Not "Very Good"

The Bible makes it abundantly clear that everything was "very good" at the end of the creation week. Six times throughout Genesis 1 we are told that God saw that what He had made was good (verses 4, 10, 12, 18, 21, 25). In verse 31, we are told that everything was "very good."

The problem is that if any of these other views is correct then God said that death, disease, bloodshed, suffering, and pain were all "good" and "very good." This is not consistent with the nature of the God of the Bible. The Bible tells us that death is the last enemy that will be destroyed (1 Cor. 15:26). As such, it could not have been a part of God's original creation. If God called these things "very good," then one must wonder if God truly is loving.

Symbiotic Relationships Non-Existent

There are countless relationships that exist between certain types of creatures in which one could not survive without the other. For example, certain plants need certain insects for pollination purposes. These same insects rely on the plant for their source of food.

If any of the above theories were correct, then plants were created millions of years before the insects. There are so many other symbiotic relationships that exist between one type of plant and one type of animal or between two types of animals. It is preposterous to believe that they survived without each other for millions of years.

Other "Order of Events" Conflicts

Inserting vast ages into the Bible's first chapter sets it at odds with modern secular scientific opinion regarding the order of events. Old-earth theory places reptiles before birds (some would claim that birds evolved from reptiles), while the Bible claims it was the other way around. Old-earthers believe that fish and sea creatures came before the land vegetation, but again, the Bible has it the other way. Old-earthers put land mammals before whales. Again, this is completely opposite of what the Bible claims. Dozens of other examples could be cited, but these are listed to show that it is impossible to add long periods of time into the biblical account without seriously damaging the doctrine of inerrancy.[2]

Conclusion

Whenever ideas foreign to Scripture are imported into it, difficulties and contradictions ensue. The Bible is self-authenticating. It does not need the help of fallible men to make it accurate. God says what He means and means what He says.

---

2. For a more complete list of the differences in the order of events, see Dr. Terry Mortenson's article at: http://www.answersingenesis.org/docs2006/0404order. asp. Accessed July 18, 2007.

Appendix C

Are There Gaps in the Genesis Genealogies?

A common argument against young-earth creationism is that gaps exist in the genealogies listed in the fifth and tenth chapters of Genesis. The old-earth proponent assumes that if gaps exist, then one cannot claim to know an approximate age of the earth based on biblical data. As a result, they say we must rely on extra-biblical sources to discover the age of the earth. Is this claim accurate? Do the genealogies actually contain gaps (open view)? Does it even matter one way or the other?

Those in favor of an old earth usually raise two pieces of evidence. First, several biblical genealogies do contain gaps. Matthew's record of Christ's genealogy is probably the most obvious. Matthew 1:8 states that Joram was the father of Uzziah, yet 1 Chronicles 3:11–14 reveals that Joram was actually the great-grandfather of Uzziah (a.k.a. Azariah). Few, if any, would dispute this point. Matthew obviously sought to organize this genealogy into groups of 14: from Abraham to David, David to Babylonian captivity, and from Babylonian captivity to Christ (Matt. 1:17). This is allowable for the Jew because it was a perfectly acceptable practice to call one's grandfather "father" or grandson, "son."

The problem with this argument is that just because some gaps exist in some genealogies does not mean that they must occur in the

Genesis genealogies. This is illogical. It commits a fallacy known as affirming the consequent. The argument goes like this: "If there are gaps in the Genesis genealogies, then we might find gaps in other genealogies. We find gaps in other genealogies; therefore, there must be gaps in the Genesis genealogies." The consequent in this argument is "we might find gaps in other genealogies." It does not follow that since this part of the argument is true, that the first statement (antecedent) is also true. Here is another argument in the exact same form to demonstrate why this conclusion is false. "If it is raining then the grass is wet. The grass is wet, therefore it must be raining." The reason that this is false is because there are other reasons why the grass may be wet. It might have dew on it or a sprinkler may be running. It might be raining, but we did not prove it by checking the grass. The same it true with the genealogies. Just because some genealogies have gaps does not prove that the Genesis genealogies have them.

The second bit of evidence seems much stronger. Genesis 11:12 states that Arphaxad begot Salah. A difficulty arises because Luke 3:36 states that Arphaxad was Salah's grandfather. According to Luke, Arphaxad was the father of Cainan, who was the father of Salah (Shelah). This seems like a watertight argument against those who believe there are no gaps (closed view). Dr. Norman Geisler certainly thinks so. He stated:

> Bishop James Ussher (1581–1656), whose chronology was used in the old Scofield Bible, argued that Adam was created 4004 B.C. However, his calculations are based on the assumption that there are no gaps in the genealogical tables of Genesis 5 and 11. But *we know this is false*.[1] (italics added)

Dr. Geisler's information concerning Ussher is correct. In fact, many scholars have "added up" the genealogies and reached a figure of approximately 4,000 years before Christ. We suggest that people should not be dogmatic on the exact date since the Bible only records the age of each person in years. It does not include months and days, so most figures could be up to a few decades off.

---

1. Norman L. Geisler, *Baker Encyclopedia of Christian Apologetics* (Grand Rapids, MI: Baker Books, 1999), p. 272.

Geisler made a bold claim concerning the "no gaps" (closed) view when he stated, "we know this is false." His primary evidence is the mention of Cainan in Luke 3:36. He goes on to make an even bolder claim concerning the open and closed views.

> If they are closed, then the creation of mankind is placed somewhere around 4000 B.C., which flies in the face of **all the historical and scientific evidence** for a minimum date for humanity[2] (bold added for emphasis).

He proceeded to argue for the open view. Dr. Geisler's statement reveals his bias. It is simply not true that "all the historical and scientific evidence" argues for a date beyond 4000 B.C. For him, the genealogies must be open because of extra-biblical information, not because of the text itself.

It may seem as though the open view is much stronger; however, this is not the case. Dr. Jonathan Sarfati has ably refuted the claims of the open view proponents by mentioning the following facts concerning Cainan in Luke 3:36:[3]

1. The extra Cainan in Genesis 11 is found only in manuscripts of the LXX[4] that were written long after Luke's gospel. The oldest LXX manuscripts do not have this extra Cainan.

2. The earliest known extant copy of Luke omits the extra Cainan. This is the 102-page (originally 144) papyrus codex of the Bodmer Collection labeled P[75] (dated between A.D. 175 and 225).

3. Josephus used the LXX as his source, but did not mention the second Cainan.

4. Julius Africanus (c. A.D. 180 – c. 250) was "the first Christian historian known to have produced a universal chronology." In

---

2. Ibid., p. 267.
3. Jonathan Sarfati, *Refuting Compromise* (Green Forest, AR: Master Books 2004), p. 296.
4. LXX is the abbreviation given to the Septuagint — the Greek translation of the Old Testament that was commonly used in New Testament times.

his chronology, written in c. A.D. 220, he also followed the LXX ages but once again omitted this mysterious Cainan.

So if Cainan was not in the original text in Luke 3:36, how did the name find its way there? The answer is quite simple. It is likely due to a copyist error, as Sarfati points out.[5] Since the phrase "the son of Cainan" (referring to the son of Enosh) appears in Luke 3:37, it is very easy to believe that a scribe accidentally copied the name twice. This is known as dittography and is a common error made by scribes.[6]

For the sake of argument, let's assume the open view is correct about the extra Cainan, which is highly unlikely considering the above information. What would this accomplish for its adherents? According to Genesis 11:12, Arphaxad was 35 years old when he begat Salah. In fact, all of the men listed from Salah to Serug were in their thirties when they had their son of record. If we must insert Cainan into the equation it will only add another 30–40 years to the age of the earth. This does not get the old-earther much closer to the tens of thousands of years required to match the alleged "facts" of history and science. Nor does it get them even close to the billions of years they need for the most-accepted age of the earth.

The Hebrew word translated as "beget" in the King James Version of the Bible is *yalad* (ילד). Although it could (in principle) indicate something more distant than a direct parent-child relationship, it is apparently never used that way in the Old Testament. That is, whenever the form "X begat Y" occurs in the Old Testament, it always indicates a direct parent-child relationship. We are aware of no exceptions. The New Testament does sometimes skip generations when using "X begat Y" as mentioned previously. But the New Testament is written in Greek, and is using a different word for "begat" (γενναω). The Old Testament "begats" (which are the ones involved in age-of-the-earth estimations) appear to be airtight — and in many cases, the surrounding passages confirm a direct parent-child relationship.

In addition, the open view proponent has failed to provide any evidence to demonstrate gaps in the Genesis 5 genealogy where the

---

5. Ibid.
6. Gleason Archer, *A Survey of Old Testament Introduction* (Chicago, IL: Moody Press, 1994), p. 60.

ages are much greater. This would certainly help their case, but the Bible rules out this possibility. Here is a list of the names in Genesis 5 and their respective ages at the birth of each one's son whose name is included in the genealogy.

Adam	130
Seth	105
Enosh	90
Cainan	70
Mahalaleel	65
Jared	162
Enoch	65
Methuselah	187
Lamech	182
Noah	500

In all, there are ten generations totaling 1,556 years at Noah's 500th year. If the open view proponent could demonstrate a gap in these genealogies, it would greatly improve his argument, but he cannot. Jude 14 tells us that Enoch was the seventh from Adam. Jude also reveals that Enoch was a prophet. This prophet gave his son Methuselah a name that means, "When he dies it shall be sent."[7] By adding up the years, we discover that Methuselah died the same year the Flood started. This biblical evidence excludes any possibility of inserting gaps into the Genesis 5 genealogies.

It seems the open view has serious problems. The first major argument is guilty of affirming the consequent and the second is not supported by historical details. The evidence is strong that the Genesis genealogies are closed. God created Adam on day 6, approximately 4,000 years before Christ. There does not seem to be any support for the notion that there are gaps in the Genesis genealogies. Even if one could be verified, it does not advance the old-earth position since it would only add a few decades or perhaps centuries, but not millions of years.

---

7. Sarfati, *Refuting Compromise*, p. 294.

Commentary on the Intelligent Design Movement

The Intelligent Design Movement (IDM) is an informal collaboration dedicated to exposing the problems with naturalistic evolution. As a movement, IDM challenges Darwinian evolution in schools, textbooks, and politics. There are some positive things about IDM but also some things that a Christian should consider carefully.

Intelligent Design Arguments

First, we must make an important distinction. The term "intelligent design" does not always refer to the Intelligent Design *Movement*. There are also, for example, intelligent design *arguments*. These arguments are used by IDM, but are also used by creationists not affiliated with IDM. Before we get into the details of IDM, it is instructive to briefly discuss intelligent design arguments, and their strengths and weaknesses.

Intelligent design arguments are those that confirm the existence of the Creator God (or at least *a* creator — not necessarily the biblical God). These arguments are based on the *teleological argument* for the existence of God. That is, living things appear to be *designed* for a function and with purpose and thus require a designer. Moreover, the universe and the earth appear to be "fine-tuned" so that life can exist. Often, intelligent design arguments draw on analogies with other things that are known to have been created by an intelligent source. Examples of intelligent design arguments would be irreducible complexity in living systems and information science arguments.

Irreducible complexity is a specific kind of order in which all the components must be in existence in order for the whole to work. A watch is the classic example. If even one of its essential parts is missing or out of place, the watch does not function properly. It is an "all-or-nothing" kind of machine. Irreducibly complex machines cannot have been generated by a gradual Darwinian process because none of the parts can work properly without all the other parts. Likewise, a living cell has many complicated parts that are interdependent; one cannot operate without all the others. Therefore, a cell cannot be the result of an evolutionary process in which parts are added one at a time. An intelligent creator is required.

Information arguments make use of the fact that, in all observed cases, creative information always comes from an intelligent source. As an example, when we read a book, we suppose that the book had an author even if we have never seen him or her. No one would assume that it was produced by a series of typos that gradually improved the quality over vast ages. Likewise, the DNA of living organisms has encoded instructions that dictate the function of every cell. Since information never comes about by chance, the reasonable deduction is that an intelligent agent created life.

These kinds of arguments (when used properly) can be very devastating to naturalistic particles-to-people evolution. However, they only indicate that life requires a creator.

They do not necessarily require *the* Creator — the God of Scripture. Intelligent design arguments would work equally well for the god of Islam or any other god. For that matter, they might lead some to believe that extraterrestrial beings are responsible for life on earth.

Intelligent design arguments therefore cannot be used to prove the existence of the biblical God. However, evidence of design is certainly consistent with the biblical God. Design is what we would expect when we accept the Bible as our starting point. Therefore, we encourage biblical creationists to use intelligent design arguments, when appropriate, as evidence that *confirms* the biblical God. Irreducible complexity and DNA packed full of information are exactly the kinds of things we would expect from biblical creation.

Both IDM supporters and young-earth creationists use intelligent design arguments. The difference is in the way these arguments are used. The IDM tends to use intelligent design arguments as their primary case against naturalistic evolution. However, we advise young-earth creationists to use the Bible as their primary source of information (Prov. 1:7), and then show how science confirms this. Logically, if the Bible is our ultimate authority (as it should be for the Christian), then it cannot be proved from something else because there is nothing more foundational.

The Intelligent Design Movement Strategy

IDM has approached the origins debate by limiting the scope of the argument to a single question: is something designed? They hope to avoid the common anti-religious bias of our culture by framing the question in a way that can be tested purely scientifically. Can we scientifically tell if something is designed by intelligence? If so, what are the characteristics we look for (such as irreducible complexity or creative information)? Whereas most public schools would never allow the Bible to be used as a source of information in a science classroom, challenges to Darwinism might be permitted on strictly scientific grounds. Those within IDM see their strategy as a way to challenge naturalistic evolution that avoids any "separation of church and state" issues.

Since IDM has limited its scope to the single question of whether something is designed, it does not endorse any particular religious view. Any person who believes in any god who created the universe or life in any way could be a member of IDM. This wedge strategy essentially divides belief about origins into two classes: naturalism and super-naturalism. By placing all super-naturalistic philosophies under the same "umbrella," IDM hopes to present a more unified front than could be done by any single religiously motivated movement.

IDM is *not* a Christian movement, although there are many Christians within the movement. Recall that IDM exists primarily to refute Darwinian evolution. It does not exist to promote Christianity or biblical creation. Those Christians within the movement may see this as a clever strategy: perhaps they think that one must first remove the stumbling block of evolution *before* a person will even consider the merits of biblical Christianity. On the surface, this certainly sounds reasonable. After all, evolution certainly can be a stumbling block to Christianity. But there are some difficulties in attempting to refute a worldview in such a piecemeal fashion.

One problem with attempting to remove evolution by scientific evidence *before* exposing a person to the Bible (as IDM does) is this: without the Bible, a person cannot properly interpret the scientific evidence. We saw in chapter 7 that the scientific method presupposes the truth of the Bible (i.e., those who employ the scientific method but deny the Bible [such as evolutionists] are being inconsistent). The real battle is not over specific scientific facts but rather how those facts should be interpreted. So, when we attempt to argue against evolution without presenting the biblical worldview, we have done nothing to address the real issue: the faulty (unbiblical) interpretive framework used by evolutionists. Attacking the evolution worldview before presenting an alternative is problematic.

Instead, we suggest that these two tasks can be done simultaneously. We can both argue for the Bible, and simultaneously argue against evolution. Remember, people think in terms of an integrated worldview, not in terms of isolated facts. Therefore, we contrast our worldview (biblical Christianity) with all its implications (creation, young earth, salvation by grace through faith, and so on) against the evolution worldview with all its implications. We show that our worldview makes sense, but that the evolution worldview is arbitrary and inconsistent with its own axioms. When we argue this way, we are using the biblical "Don't Answer, Answer" strategy indicated in Proverbs 26:4–5.

The Intelligent Design Movement does not employ this biblical strategy. The evolutionist insists that the Bible is not a reliable source of information. Those in IDM accept this standard (even if they don't actually believe that way) and attempt to argue by the evolutionists' criteria. However, we must not "answer the fool according to his folly"[1] lest we be like him. Instead, the consistent Christian stands on the authority of the Bible. We would only stand on another authority in principle for the sake of argument to show how ridiculous it is.

We understand that there are certain times and places where it may not be appropriate to explicitly mention the Bible. For example, in a public high school, a teacher may be forbidden to teach students about the Bible in a biology class. (This just shows how far our society has gone "downhill." After all, the Bible is the basis for biology, and all science as we saw in chapter 7.) Still, even when we cannot explicitly mention the Bible, we never stand on any other authority in practice. Instead we challenge other (false) authorities by showing that when one stands on them (in principle) it leads to nonsense — thus "answering the fool according to his folly lest he be wise in his own eyes." We can, for example, show that old-earth assumptions (such as naturalism and uniformitarianism) lead to conclusions that refute an old earth. This approach is commonly used in young-earth arguments as shown in chapter 7.

The Unknown God

Since IDM is not a Christian movement, we would not expect that its goals and methods would always match with those of a Christian (though there may be some overlap). IDM seeks to persuade our culture that there is a creator. This is true, of course, but the Christian must not be content to end there. As Christians, our desire is to think and act in accordance with God's will. It is our wish that none "should perish, but that all should come to repentance" (2 Pet. 3:9). So, we don't simply want to persuade people that there is a god who created life. We want to see people brought to saving faith in Christ, our Creator and Savior.

In Acts 17:22–31, Paul observed that the men of Athens were very religious. But they did not have a saving knowledge of Christ. They had erected an altar to "the unknown god." Paul was not content to leave them to their belief in *a* god. Instead, He declared to them who

---

1. Here we are not referring to any specific person as a fool. Rather we are using biblical language to describe a biblical strategy. See chapters 7 and 8 for a more complete discussion of Proverbs 26:4–5.

God is. He began in Genesis, declaring that God is the Creator of all things. By quoting many of their sayings, Paul pointed out that they knew God already[2] and had been borrowing from the Christian worldview. Paul did not end his sermon on creation until he told them about the resurrection of Christ — the culmination of the gospel. Although some mocked Paul (Acts 17:32), others wanted to hear more, and some believed (Acts 17:34). Paul's sermon was very successful considering that he was speaking to an "evolutionized" culture that rejected the Bible. Paul followed the "Don't Answer, Answer" strategy; he simultaneously refuted the unbelieving worldview while defending the Christian worldview.

The Pretended Neutrality Fallacy

It is quite common these days for evolutionists to demand that we argue on their terms. In particular, we are told that we must "leave the Bible out of it." After all, the evolutionist does not believe the Bible (at least not Genesis 1), so he claims that it would not be fair to use the Bible. We must meet on "neutral ground." On the surface this seems reasonable, and many Christians are therefore inclined to leave the Bible out of the discussion. But is this really meeting on neutral ground?

The idea that the Bible is not reliable when talking about origins is a *secular* idea. After all, the consistent Christian believes the Bible is indeed reliable. The notion that the Bible should not be used when discussing origins is not a "neutral" idea. It is a secular idea. Too many Christians have been duped into arguing on secular terms.

We must always remember that the Bible is our ultimate authority. Since the Bible has demonstrated itself to be accurate on all matters upon which it touches, it is not the Christian who is "foolish" for standing on the Word but rather the non-Christian who is foolish for abandoning it. If an evolutionist insists that he will not start from the Bible — that's *his* problem. Don't make it yours! He is the one who is arbitrarily rejecting well-established recorded history in favor of guesswork.

Biblically, there is no such thing as "neutral ground" when it comes to one's ultimate authority. In Luke 11:20, Jesus says, "He who is not

---

2. Romans 1:18–20 indicates that God has made himself known to everyone. So, there is no excuse for those who suppress the truth about God.

with Me is against Me" and in Mark 9:40 "For he who is not against us is on our side." Therefore, the claim that there is a neutral ground between the believer and unbeliever is itself unbiblical. By saying that there is such a thing as neutral ground, the unbeliever has already taken the position that the Bible is wrong — at least on that point. Thus, the unbeliever is really only *pretending* to be neutral, and so this is called the "pretended neutrality fallacy."[3] If the Christian agrees to these terms, he has already lost, because he has agreed that the Bible is wrong. By "answering the fool according to his folly," the believer has become like him in the sense that he rejects Scripture as his starting point.

The Intelligent Design Movement as a strategy agrees to secular terms for debating. It leaves the Bible out of the discussion, avoids appealing to the biblical God, and avoids any reference to biblical history or the biblical time scale. We have seen the problems with this approach. Instead, we encourage Christians to follow the biblical strategy outlined in Proverbs 26:4–5. Do not stand on any authority other than the Bible, except for the sake of argument to show how foolish it would be.

No World History

Since IDM does not use the Bible in any way, it has no history to account for the present world. The evolution model at least has a history (albeit an incorrect one) that allegedly accounts for the present world. Evolutionists claim that they can explain the fossil record, rock formations, mountains, and canyons with their model. Moreover, biblical (i.e., young-earth) creationists also have a historical model that can account for these things. The ability of a model to explain various features of the world is a powerful asset. But IDM has no specific history (as a movement) and therefore does not even attempt to explain many features of the present world.

IDM has been criticized for this. But it cannot have a history because it doesn't represent any specific worldview. Some evolutionists have argued that IDM is deceptive because the Christians within it are

---

3. This kind of fallacy has been addressed by Dr. Greg Bahnsen. Dr. Bahnsen had a tremendous gift for being able to articulate biblical truths particularly in matters of logical argumentation. These concepts are addressed in Dr. Bahnsen's book *Always Ready* (Nacogdoches, TX: Covenant Media Press, 1996).

not upfront about their worldview. Critics of IDM have argued that it is a "backdoor" method of attempting to get the Bible into schools.

Since IDM has no history, it is perfectly compatible with old-earth creationism. Indeed, many individuals within IDM are old-earth creationists. They have accepted the secular view of history such as the big bang and the secular view of the geologic column and as a result have inherited the many problems and inconsistencies addressed in this book. Of course, some members of IDM are young-earth creationists, but they see IDM as a better strategy than being upfront about their worldview in its entirety.

Designed for Pain

There is a common argument for evolution that deserves mention here because it is very effective against IDM. This is a variation of the "problem of pain." Namely, there are certain features of living organisms that appear to be designed to cause pain. Examples of this are thorns, bee stings, parasitic organisms, and carnivorous activity. Evolutionists argue that a good God would not have designed such things. Such features make more sense in an evolutionary world "red in tooth and claw." This argument is particularly effective against Christians within the IDM because Christians argue that their Creator is a God of love.

Biblical creationists are able to answer this objection quite easily. God is good and He did originally make a perfect world without any pain or bloodshed. But today, the world is cursed because of man's sin. God no longer upholds the universe in a perfect fashion (Rom. 8:20–22) as He did in the beginning. Therefore, many things in the present world have deteriorated from what they once were. Mutations (mistakes in the genome) can cause disease and suffering. But not all of the bad things in the world today are the result of mere gradual deterioration; God actively judged the world in response to Adam's rebellion. Thorns in particular are specifically mentioned as being a result of the curse (Gen. 3:18). Since God instituted the curse, we would expect that some things in today's world are designed to be painful. We would expect that other things cause pain due to deterioration. But since IDM does not appeal to biblical history, its supporters cannot answer the objection of pain.

Biblical Authority

So, despite the positive aspects of IDM, there are clearly many difficulties with it as well. All these problems directly or indirectly come back to the issue of ultimate authority. Each of us must either start with the Bible as our ultimate authority, or autonomous human reasoning. But since all knowledge is in Christ (Col. 2:3), autonomous reasoning does not lead to truth (Prov. 1:7, 14:12, 16:25). In fact, the only reason that unbelievers are able to know anything is because they are not completely consistent in their rejection of biblical authority. We could not reason in a completely autonomous fashion even if we tried — we would still have to borrow God's laws of logic in order to deduce anything.

Relying on God's Word as our foundation for reasoning does not mean that we need to accept things on "blind faith." God certainly expects us to think and reason. But our thinking must have a foundation — we have to start somewhere. Without the foundation of the Bible, we would have no place to even begin our reasoning. We must learn to build our worldview on the rock of God's Word, not the shifting sands of human opinions (Matt. 7:24–27).

The Intelligent Design Movement does not rely on the Bible as its ultimate authority. But then again, IDM is not a Christian movement, so this isn't surprising. We certainly commend those in IDM for challenging Darwinian evolution and naturalism in general. We would encourage those Christians with ties to IDM to think carefully about the points that have been raised in this section, and to consider the biblical strategy of Proverbs 26:4–5. We encourage all Christians to be biblically minded about all things, placing their confidence not in man's autonomy, but in God's Word.

The Big-Bang God or the God of Scripture?

S ome people have suggested that God (or *a* god) used a "big bang" to create the universe. The big bang is the secular model of how the universe formed. However, the consistent Christian has no need to speculate on how and when God might have created the universe. The Creator himself has left a written record that summarizes His creative acts — a record that contradicts the big-bang model on many points. Sadly, many people are inclined to ignore what God has said about what He did. Instead, they rely on secular philosophy to reconstruct a past that contradicts the recorded history and eyewitness testimony of the Bible.

Can you imagine if people applied such thinking to other fields of study? What if someone rejected recorded history and claimed that World War I never happened because his philosophy does not allow for the possibility of a world war. Would this be reasonable? These days, it is common for people to reject the possibility of a supernatural, biblical creation simply because they embrace the philosophy of naturalism — the belief that "nature is all that there is."

Naturalism and uniformitarianism are the driving philosophies behind the big bang. That is, the big-bang model attempts to describe the formation of the entire universe by processes currently operating within the universe. Stars, planets, and galaxies are all said to have formed "naturalistically" — by the laws of nature currently in operation. The expansion of the universe is assumed to be naturalistic and uniformitarian in the big-bang model.

In chapter 7, we explored the errors of naturalistic and uniformitarian thinking, and how such notions lead to incorrect conclusions. The big bang is simply one of many incorrect conclusions derived from secular assumptions. It is not compatible with the Bible. Therefore, Christians should reject it. Let's summarize a few of the differences.

The big bang accepts the secular order of events, not the biblical order (see Appendix B). For example, stars come before the earth in the big bang, but the order is reversed in the Bible. The big bang teaches that the universe is billions of years old, whereas the Bible teaches only thousands of years. The big bang teaches that the first stars formed by natural processes, but the Bible teaches that God made the stars (Gen. 1:14–16).

The big bang is really just a story about the alleged past. But few people realize that it is also a story about the alleged future. The big-bang model (in the most accepted variation) claims that our universe will expand forever and usable energy will eventually all be converted to a useless form; no life will be possible at that point. It's a bleak outlook, and one that is vastly different from the Bible's description of the future. Scripture teaches that there will be a resurrection, judgment, and then a restoration of paradise. Clearly, the Bible is not compatible with the big bang. Unfortunately, too few Christians realize the many contradictions between the big-bang story and the recorded history of the Bible.

Jumping on the Big-Bang Bandwagon

It is becoming increasingly popular for apologetics ministries to cite the big-bang theory as evidence or proof for the existence of God. This is not necessarily a new phenomenon, since Dr. Hugh Ross has been doing this for years in his lectures, books, and website. Unfortunately, it seems to be gaining momentum and many well-known apologists are falling for it, including John Ankerberg, Lee

Strobel, and Norman Geisler. There are several problems with this approach.

First, there is a real danger in claiming that the Bible is consistent with the big bang (or worse — to say, as some do, that the Bible *teaches* the big bang). The Bible is the Word of God and does not change. The big-bang theory changes regularly. Dr. Ross used to claim that the universe was 17 billion years old (give or take 3 billion years).[1] In 2004, Ross claimed that scientists now know the universe is 13.7 billion years old — this is 300 million years outside of his previous "known" range. In addition, many astronomers have posited different ages for the universe ranging from 7–20 billion years. So which one does the Bible "teach"? Ross is forced to reinterpret the Bible every time the theory changes.

Second, the big-bang theory does not provide evidence for the God of the Bible. At best, the big bang posits a beginning to the universe and

---

1. Cited by Mark Van Bebber and Paul S. Taylor in *Creation and Time* (Mesa, AZ: Eden Communications, 1994), p. 109.

therefore, a cause. However, that cause need not be divine. Carl Sagan and Isaac Asimov popularized the oscillating universe idea,[2] in which the cause is a previous universe. So the big bang in no way proves the biblical account. The Muslim could make the exact same claim. So does the big-bang theory support the belief that Allah created everything?

Third, the Bible does not need us to invent or use fallacious evidence to support its claims. In fact, the Bible warns against following such concepts based on human reasoning rather than God's Word (Col. 2:8). There is enough scientific evidence to confirm the Bible without adding the big-bang theory to the mix. What happens if and/or when scientists stop believing in the big-bang theory and come up with a new theory? A number of scientists are already doing just that![3]

Finally, and most importantly, the Bible just does *not* support the big-bang theory nor does the big-bang theory support the Bible. They are contradictory on many issues. Those who claim that the big bang (or any other old-earth ideas) supports the Bible are unwittingly misleading the Church in this area. Consider the following examples.

First, in his *Systematic Theology: Volume One,* Norman Geisler makes the following claims:

a) The Bible teaches that everything came into existence in the "exact order that modern science" has discovered. He goes on to list this order: "the universe came first, then the earth, then the land and sea. After this came life in the sea, then land animals, and finally, last of all, human beings."[4] Actually, the Bible states that the sea was created before the land. Other

---

2. This view states that a series of big bangs occurs every 20–100 billion years and that the universe is eternal. In the past, this view was largely abandoned due to thermodynamic problems. However, a version of this model has regained some support more recently. Philosophically, this view fails because if matter were eternal, then an infinite number of days would have to be traversed before today. It is impossible to traverse an infinite number of days; therefore, there must be a beginning and a Beginner to "begin" the universe.

3. The reader is again referred to the paper mentioned in chapter 1. It is available at <http://www.cosmologystatement.org>.

4. Norman L. Geisler, *Systematic Theology: Volume One* (Minneapolis, MN: Bethany House, 2002), p. 545.

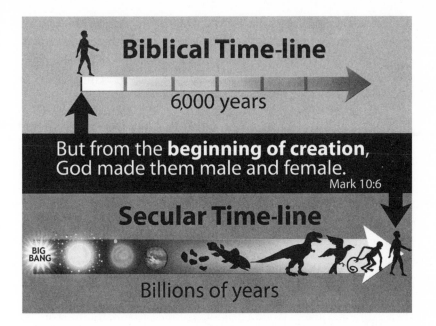

than that discrepancy, the Bible certainly does teach this order. Nevertheless, Geisler's comments are misleading. First, when the Bible teaches that "God created the heavens and the earth" (Gen 1:1), this does not include the sun, moon, and stars since these were made on the fourth day (Gen 1:14–19). The big-bang adherents teach that the sun evolved before the earth, while the Bible teaches that the earth came first. Second, Geisler conveniently leaves out the creation of the flying creatures on the fifth day. This contradicts the evolutionary belief of many scientists since they believe birds evolved from land animals (reptiles). There is no way to reconcile this with the biblical account without ignoring or twisting Scripture.

b) On pages 300–301 of the same book, Geisler implies that belief in a six-day creation is tantamount to believing that the sun orbits the earth. He cites Martin Luther's argument as an example. Luther wrongly believed in a geocentric solar system and used Joshua's account of the long day (Josh. 10:12) as evidence. However, neither Joshua nor any other biblical author makes a statement that undoubtedly teaches geocentricity. Geisler proceeds to add one of Luther's comments about a six-day creation as if this is as erroneous as believing in geocentricity. Not only is this a case of comparing apples to oranges, it is misleading because it assumes that science has proven a six-day creation to be wrong — which it has not.

Second, Dr. Hugh Ross has made the claim that life *could not* exist unless the universe was about 14 billion years old.[5] Yet Dr. Ross is well aware that the Bible teaches that one day God will create new heavens and a new earth. He does not believe this will take billions of years to create. If God can and will create this new place instantaneously (or at least in a short time) then why could He not do this with the original creation? Such inconsistent thinking is typical of old-earth theology. Dr. Ross routinely places limits on God that God has not placed on himself. Dr. Ross claims that the "transcendent Creator is at least a trillion, trillion, trillion, trillion, trillion, trillion, trillion, trillion times more intelligent than the people at Cal Tech."[6] While this sounds impressive, it is demeaning to the God who is *infinitely* more intelligent than any person. Those who believe in a young earth are often ridiculed for limiting God; however, the shoe is actually on the other foot. We limit ourselves to taking God at His Word. According to Dr. Ross, it is impossible for God to have created everything in six days of approximately 24 hours each — even though His Word clearly teaches that He did. One is reminded of Jesus' statement in Matthew 22:29, "You are mistaken, not knowing the Scriptures nor the power of God." Who is really placing limits on God?

The Bible does not imply or teach the big-bang theory. In fact, the Bible and the big bang teach the opposite on nearly every major event

5. He made this claim in a debate with Dr. Kent Hovind on the *John Ankerberg Show* and also at the Intelligent Design 2004 Conference in Highlands, North Carolina, in June 2004. Ironically, in 1996, Ross told a chapel session at Dallas Theological Seminary that "it only works in a cosmos of a hundred-billion trillion stars that's precisely sixteen-billion-years old."

6. Dr. Ross stated this at the ID 2004 Conference. See previous footnote for details.

of history. The Bible teaches very plainly that God created everything in the span of six literal days of approximately 24 hours each (Gen. 1; Exod. 20:11, 31:17–18). Any attempt to compromise this teaching produces serious theological errors, as shown in Appendix B. Christians need to learn to trust in God's Word because "it is better to trust in the Lord than to put confidence in man" (Ps. 118:8). God says what He means and means what He says — let's not add man's fallible and changing opinions to His perfect Word.

What about the Scientific Evidence?

Many people don't realize that the big bang is not only bad theology, but it is bad science as well. Is the big bang the same kind of science that put men on the moon, or allows your computer to function? Not at all. The big bang isn't testable, repeatable laboratory science. It doesn't make specific predictions that are later confirmed by observation and experimentation. In fact, the big bang is at odds with a number of principles of real operational science. Let's explore just a few of these.

One significant issue is the problem of the "missing monopoles." A "monopole" is a hypothetical massive particle that is just like a magnet, but with only one pole. So, a monopole would have either a "north" pole, or a "south" pole, but not both. Particle physicists claim that magnetic monopoles should have been created in the high temperature conditions of the big bang. Since monopoles are predicted to be stable, they should have lasted to this day. Yet, despite considerable search efforts, monopoles have not been found. Where are the monopoles? The fact that we don't find any monopoles suggests that the universe never was that hot; this indicates that there never was a big bang. But it's perfectly consistent with the Bible's account of creation, since the universe did not start at extremely high temperatures.

Consider the "baryon number problem." The big bang supposes that matter (hydrogen and helium gas) was created from energy as the universe expanded. However, experimental physics tells us that whenever matter is created from energy, such a reaction also produces *antimatter*. Antimatter has similar properties to matter, except the charges of the particles are reversed. (So whereas a proton has a positive charge, an anti-proton has a *negative* charge.) In any reaction where energy is transformed into matter, it produces an exactly equal amount of anti-matter; there are no known exceptions.

The big bang (which has no matter to begin with — only energy) should have produced precisely equal amounts of matter and antimatter. Thus, if the big bang were true, there should be an exactly equal amount of matter and antimatter in the universe today. But there is not. The visible universe is comprised almost entirely of matter — with only trace amounts of antimatter anywhere.

Additionally, there are many lines of evidence that indicate the universe is much younger than billions of years. Spiral galaxies are an example of this. These galaxies rotate differentially — meaning the inner portions rotate faster than the outer portions. So the spiral structure is constantly becoming tighter and tighter. If these galaxies were really billions of years old, they would be so twisted up that the spiral structure could not be seen. But we do see countless numbers of spiral galaxies — indicating they are much younger than the big bang teaches.

What to Make of the Scientific Problems

Of course, big-bang supporters often propose various solutions to these problems. These "rescuing devices" attempt to save the big-bang model from all the contrary evidence. These hypotheses have problems of their own, for which there are proposed solutions (which themselves have problems and so on). For example, the "spiral density wave" hypothesis is supposed to preserve the spiral structure of galaxies to accommodate the big-bang time scale, but is inconsistent with the magnetic fields that permeate galaxies, for which another hypothesis must be invoked.

So, the problems listed above (and many others that were not included in this book) are not to be taken as "proofs" that the big bang is wrong. Big-bang supporters can always invoke a rescuing device. It is the Bible that proves the big bang wrong. The scientific problems with the big bang merely confirm this. They are symptomatic of the fact that the big bang is not true.

In fact, in order for science to be possible, biblical creation must be true. We saw in chapter 7 how the Bible alone provides the necessary preconditions for scientific analysis. Only if there is a God who is beyond time and who upholds the universe in a consistent fashion (the future universe operates like the past universe) can the testable/repeatable nature of the scientific method make any sense. Yet, God's promise to uphold the future as He has the past is given in the Book of Genesis. Specifically, Genesis 8:22 tells us that there are certain cycles we can count on in the future. Only biblical creation explains why we have an orderly, logical universe and minds that can interpret that universe. Without the straightforward teachings of the Bible (and Genesis in particular), what basis would we have for the uniformity we see in nature? Without biblical creation, what right would we have to expect that science is even possible?

By attempting to use science to support his case, the big-bang supporter has actually philosophically destroyed his own position. The big-bang supporter may attempt to argue that science refutes biblical (young-earth) creation, but he is using something (science) that makes no sense without biblical creation. In order for his scientific argument to make sense, it would necessarily have to be wrong. Science cannot exist apart from its foundation: the biblical God. And so the big bang is nothing more than an exercise in unbiblical, vain philosophy — the kind the Bible warns us about in Colossians 2:8.

Conclusions

There simply is no rational reason to believe in the big bang. It is not compatible with the Bible, and it's not good science. We have sampled just a few of the scientific difficulties with the big bang. Although secular astronomers have proposed potential solutions to such problems, we suggest that such problems are symptomatic of the underlying incorrect worldview. The big bang erroneously assumes that the universe was *not* supernaturally created, but that it came about by natural processes. However, reality does not comport with this notion. Science confirms the message of the Bible: "In the beginning, God created the heaven and the earth."

Recommended Reading for Further Research

Archaeology & Anthropology

Dr. Jack Cuozzo, *Buried Alive* (Green Forest, AR: Master Books, 1998).

Duane Gish, *Evolution: The Fossils Still Say No!* (San Diego, CA: Creation-Life Publishers, 1979).

Marvin Lubenow, *Bones of Contention* (Grand Rapids, MI: Baker Book House, 1992).

Astronomy

Dr. Don DeYoung, *Astronomy and the Bible: Questions and Answers* (Grand Rapids, MI: Baker Books, 2000).

Dr. Danny Faulkner, *Universe by Design* (Green Forest, AR: Master Books, 2004).

Dr. D. Russell Humphreys, *Starlight and Time* (Green Forest, AR: Master Books, 1994).

Dr. Jason Lisle, *Taking Back Astronomy* (Green Forest, AR: Master Books, 2006).

Alex Williams and Dr. John Hartnett, *Dismantling the Big Bang* (Green Forest, AR: Master Books, 2005).

Biology

Ken Ham, *One Blood* (Green Forest, AR: Master Books, 1999).

Dr. Henry Morris and Dr. Gary Parker, *What is Creation Science?* (Green Forest, AR: Master Books, 1982).

John Woodmorappe, *Noah's Ark: A Feasibility Study* (Santee, CA: Institute for Creation Research, 1996).

Geology

Dr. Steven Austin, *Grand Canyon: Monument to Catastrophe* (Santee, CA: Institute for Creation Research, 1994).

Dr. Henry Morris and Dr. John Whitcomb, *The Genesis Flood* (Philadelphia, PA: Presbyterian and Reformed Publishing Co., 1961).

Dr. John Morris, *The Young Earth* (Green Forest, AR: Master Books, 1994).

Dr. Terry Mortenson, *The Great Turning Point* (Green Forest, AR: Master Books, 2004).

Tom Vail, *Grand Canyon: A Different View* (Green Forest, AR: Master Books, 2003).

Dr. John Woodmorappe, *Studies in Flood Geology* (El Cajon, CA: Institute for Creation Research, 1999).

Dating Methods

Dr. Don DeYoung, *Thousands . . . Not Billions* (Green Forest, AR: Master Books, 2005).

Dr. John Woodmorappe, *The Mythology of Modern Dating Methods* (El Cajon, CA: Institute for Creation Research, 1999).

Apologetics and the Philosophy of Science

Dr. Greg Bahnsen, *Always Ready* (Nacogdoches, TX: Covenant Media Press, 1996).

Dr. Greg Bahnsen, *Pushing the Antithesis* (Powder Springs, GA: American Vision, 2007).

Miscellaneous

Dr. Werner Gitt, *In the Beginning Was Information* (Green Forest, AR: Master Books, 2006).

Dr. Henry Morris and Dr. John Morris, *The Modern Creation Trilogy* (especially Volume II) (Green Forest, AR: Master Books, 1996).

Michael Oard, *Frozen in Time* (Green Forest, AR: Master Books, 2004).

Dr. Jonathan Sarfati, *Refuting Evolution* (Green Forest, AR: Master Books, 1999); *Refuting Evolution 2* (Green Forest, AR: Master Books, 2002); and *Refuting Compromise* (Green Forest, AR: Master Books, 2004).

About the authors

Tim Chaffey lives in southwestern Wisconsin with his wife, Casey, and two children, Kayla and Judah.

He has taught Bible and science classes at the junior and senior high levels for the past six years. He also served as a pastor for four years. He holds a BS and MA in biblical and theological studies. He has earned a Master of Divinity degree specializing in theology and apologetics at Liberty Baptist Theological Seminary.

Tim is the founder and director of Midwest Apologetics (www.midwestapologetics.org). The ministry is located near Dubuque, Iowa, and is dedicated to upholding and defending the Word of God from the beginning to the end. To accomplish this goal, Tim speaks at various churches, camps, and schools on a variety of topics. Please visit the website for a list of available talks and for booking information.

Jason Lisle is a research scientist and speaker with Answers in Genesis Ministries. He holds a bachelor's degree in physics and astronomy from Ohio Wesleyan University, and a master's degree and PhD in astrophysics from the University of Colorado in Boulder. Dr. Lisle is also the planetarium director at the Creation Museum, and has written several of the programs now available, including "The Created Cosmos" and "Worlds of Creation."

Dr. Lisle has written extensively on the topics of creation and astronomy, in secular and creation literature. He is author of the book *Taking Back Astronomy*, and is a coauthor of *The New Answers Book* volumes I and II. For more information on Dr. Lisle, including his speaking schedule and information on the latest planetarium shows at the Creation Museum, visit www.answersingenesis.org.

The New Answers Book
Ken Ham, General Editor

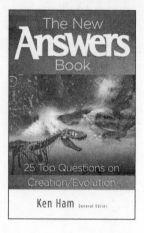

An essential resource for any believer, *The New Answers Book* addresses some of the most difficult questions that Christians face today. Perfect for personal use or group study, this version of one of the most popular creation science titles ever published is the product of multiple revisions with over 300,000 in print. Easy to understand answers for your questions on archaeology and the Bible, the Ice Age, "races" of man, and creation. *The New Answers Book* gives you the information you need to defend your faith!

paperback • 360 pages • $14.99
ISBN-13: 978-0-89051-509-9 • ISBN-10: 0-89051-509-3

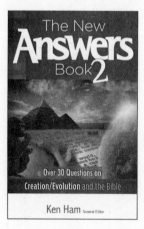

The New Answers Book 2
Ken Ham, General Editor

What happens when you have more "hot" questions on the Bible and creationism than you can answer in one book? You create a second volume! *The New Answers Book: Volume 2* explores over 30 exciting and faith-affirming topics, including:

- The fall of Lucifer and the origin of evil
- When does life begin (and why does it matter)?
- Is evolution a religion (and why should I care)?
- Archaeology, Egyptian chronology, and the Great Flood
- Could early biblical figures really live to over 900 years?
- What was the star of Bethlehem?

paperback • 378 pages • $14.99
ISBN-13: 978-0-89051-537-2 • ISBN-10: 0-89051-537-9

Available at Christian bookstores nationwide